47366

Middle-Class Couples

Hope cannot aim at making the mutilated social character of women identical to the mutilated social character of men; rather, its goal must be a state in which the face of the grieving woman disappears simultaneously with that of the bustling, capable man, a state in which all that survives the disgrace of the difference between the sexes is the happiness that difference makes possible.

(Theodor W. Adorno, *Prisms*, Spearman London, 1967, page 82)

Middle-Class Couples

A Study of Segregation, Domination and Inequality in Marriage

STEPHEN EDGELL
University of Salford

London
GEORGE ALLEN & UNWIN
Boston   Sydney

GEORGE ALLEN & UNWIN LTD
40 Museum Street, London WC1A 1LU

©George Allen & Unwin (Publishers) Ltd, 1980

British Library Cataloguing in Publication Data

Edgell, Stephen R
  Middle-class couples.
  1. Marriage — Great Britain
  2. Middle classes — Great Britain
  I. Title
  301'.42   HQ614   79-41409

  ISBN 0-04-301109-8

Typeset in 10 on 11 point Times by Red Lion Setters, Holborn, London
and printed in Great Britain
by Biddles Ltd, Guildford, Surrey

Contents

Tables

To Avi and Jones

Preface

This book is a revised and shortened version of my doctoral thesis. At different stages of the research I have benefited from discussions with many people. At the risk of invidious comparison I would particularly like to place on record my thanks to Alan Stanton for sustaining a high level of critical interest and encouragement over such a long period of time. In the same context I would also like to mention the following: Lorraine Barić, Colin Bell, David Bennett, Nicky Hart, David Morgan, Jeff Porter, Joel Richman and Christopher Turner. Needless to say I also owe a great debt to all those who helped in the acquisition of a sample and all those who agreed to participate but have to remain anonymous. Finally, the manuscript was efficiently and expeditiously typed by Penny Kay.

CHAPTER 1
Introduction

The research reported in this book looks critically at the view that 'middle-class' marriages in contemporary Britain are characterised by role desegregation and equality: a view that seemed to be heavily influenced by Parsonian functionalist theory and to be based on very little, or inadequate empirical data. To the extent that professional workers and their wives are part of the 'middle class', the observation made by Klein as long ago as 1965, and reiterated since by many others (for example, Pahl and Pahl, 1971, p. 15), that 'very few sociological descriptions' are available on this section of the social class structure, compared to studies of the 'working-class' family, remains largely true today. My initial response to this situation was to try and clarify some of the issues by examining the then available literature.

The first problem was the familiar one of focus and definition. In view of the heterogeneity of the 'middle classes' I decided to concentrate my attention on the less ambiguous category of professional workers. However, this apparently more clear-cut group contains an increasing variety of occupations and may itself be subdivided into self-employed and salaried professionals. This distinction is historically important and is comparable to a number of other dichotomies, notably locals and cosmopolitans, traditionalists and non-traditionalists, spiralists and burgesses. In the light of the growth of salaried professionals in Britain and elsewhere in this century (Routh, 1965), I decided to restrict myself in the first instance to an analysis of the conjugal role relationships of salaried professional workers and their wives.

The concept that most explicitly covers the characteristic mobility experiences associated with professional employment in a bureaucracy is spiralism. This term refers to 'the progressive ascent of specialists . . . through a series of higher positions in one or more hierarchical structures with a concomitant residential mobility through a number of communities' (Watson, 1964, p. 147). Spiralists were contrasted by Watson with another social group that he called burgesses. This category includes 'shopkeepers, owners and managers of small-scale industries, and other small capitalists, whose limited scale of operations usually restricts them to a specific local community'. Self-employed professional workers such as doctors, dentists and solicitors also come into this category, although their possession of specialised educational qualifications means that unlike other kinds of burgesses they retain a latent spatial mobility potential. Whilst Watson had studied the social significance of spiralists and burgesses for residential communities, and Bell (1968a) had studied their social and kinship networks, there had been no empirical research into their marital relationships.

The precise nature of my interest was further clarified by consideration of the family life-cycle. In the work of Bott (1971) this factor had been held constant. Bott had limited her study to 'families with children under 10 years of age' on the grounds that 'this phase is considered to be one of the most crucial in family development' (Bott, 1971, p. 11). However, in a footnote to this passage, Bott had suggested that 'it would be interesting to study families differing in phase but similar in socioeconomic status'. Since I was interested in couples characterised by similar occupational and socioeconomic circumstances, it was unnecessary to be as restrictive as Bott. Consequently, I decided to focus my attention on spiralist (professional) families at the child-rearing stage of the family cycle and, following Bell (1968b), defined this stage as lasting from the birth of the first child to the marriage of the first child.

My initial review of the relevant literature suggested that the conjugal role relationships of spiralists were affected by a variety of influences that could be reduced to two groups. One group of influences seemed to favour work-centredness, husband domination and segregated conjugal roles; the other group favoured home-centredness, egalitarianism and joint conjugal roles. More specifically it was hypothesised that 'the resolution of the conflicting forces that impinge upon spiralists at the child-rearing stage of the family cycle will be related to their orientation to success at work' (Edgell, 1970, p. 318). The possible interrelationships between work careers and family life developed in this paper on the basis of research material gathered by others in projects with differing objectives clearly required empirical investigation.

In the beginning, therefore, the intention was to collect data specifically on the conjugal role relationships of spiralists at the child-rearing stage of the family cycle. The second aim was to understand why the patterns of conjugal role behaviour and culture, so described, prevail. These twin objectives are common to most sociological research and have been succinctly expressed by Nisbet: 'To discover the essential data of social behaviour and the connection among the data is the first objective of sociology. To explain the data and the connections is the second and larger objective' (1970, p. 5).

Arising out of these first two aims, a third and more critical part of the research process is to question existing knowledge. As far as this study is concerned, the main targets were inevitably those authors who had hitherto been the most influential in the sociological study of the family in general and the relationship between the family and work in particular: in other words, Parsons and his functionalist model and Bott, whose research is in many ways an attempt to extend Parsonian theory into the world of empirical data. Thus Bott replaces Parsons's emphasis on the universal trend towards the increasing structural isolation of the conjugal family due to the economic system's need for social and spatial mobility, with an analysis of 'variability' (1971, p. 102). Bott found that the industrial system did not have the same effect on all families. Consequently, the degree of isolation varied and with it the patterning of conjugal role relationships. A critical analysis of Parsons's abstract general theory of the family and modern society and Bott's empirically grounded variant is combined with a more substantive concern for the related issues of sexual equality and role segregation. Until quite recently, the conventional wisdom seems to have been that since the nineteenth century an increase in sex role desegregation and a decline in male authority has occurred in Western societies. After reviewing research undertaken in Britain, Dennis concluded that sex roles inside and outside marriage are becoming 'indistinct' and 'interchangeable' and that there is a 'movement towards greater equality between spouses. The wife comes to have more say in all phases of family life' (1962, p. 88). These trends are thought by some to have gone furthest among 'middle-class' couples. For example, two of the most explicit statements to this effect are:

> Today in middle-class America, authority in matters economic and familial is shared by husband and wife, decisions are made jointly, and the accent is on companionship. The patriarchal family is being replaced by the equalitarian family.
> (Ogburn and Nimkoff, 1955, p. 179)

> It seems to be generally true in our society that as one proceeds down the social scale the sex roles become more sharply defined and more rigidly typed.   (Newson and Newson, 1963, p. 219)

The patriarchal type of family, 'with its division of functions between a providing and protective father and a home-making, submissive mother' may be regarded as obsolete (Myrdal and Klein, 1968, p. 160) and even with abhorrence among 'better-educated' men and women (Goode, 1970, pp. 58-9, 373). However, the material presented in this study strongly suggests otherwise. In advancing the view that subordination still characterises the situation of most women, it is in no way implied that this is unique to industrial capitalism or to the current stage of development of that type of society. Lack of sexual equality has been widely reported in both industrial and non-industrial societies, and in capitalist and socialist societies (Veblen, 1899; Marx, 1970; Horoszowski, 1971a and 1971b; Engels, 1972; Hamilton, 1978).[1]

The issue of sexual equality has experienced something of a belated political and sociological revival in liberal, democratic, industrial, capitalist societies, no doubt to the surprise of certain sociologists.[2] The realisation that only limited progress has been made in the direction of full sexual equality in society and that inequality characterises most aspects of marriage are two of the central points of this study of professional workers and their wives at the child-rearing stage of the family life-cycle.

Notes: Chapter 1

1 There are also cases of minor and temporary deviations to this almost universal tendency. For example, during the early period of the introduction of the factory system in England, it was often easier for women (and children) to obtain employment than men (Thompson, 1968; Smelser, 1972; Rowbotham, 1974). For a time this development usurped the power of many working-class husbands and led Engels to observe that: 'This condition, which unsexes the man and takes from woman all womanliness without being able to bestow upon the man true womanliness, or the woman true manliness—this condition which degrades, in the most shameful way, both sexes, and, through them, Humanity, is the last result of our much-praised civilisation, the final achievement of all the efforts and struggles of hundreds of generations to improve their own situation and that of their posterity. We must either despair of mankind, and its aims and efforts, when we see all our labour and toil result in such a mockery, or we must admit that all human society has hitherto sought salvation in a false direction; we must admit that so total a reversal of the position of the sexes can have come to pass only because the sexes have been placed in a false position from the beginning. If the reign of the wife over the husband, as inevitably brought about by the factory system, is inhuman, the pristine rule of the husband over the wife must have been inhuman too' (1962, p. 179).

2 For example, J. A. and Olive Banks have written that 'organised feminist movements, if they continue at all today, can be counted alongside vegetarianism and nudism as bordering on the cult . . . a movement which has few adherents today' (1964, pp. 548-9). In other respects, this article was one of the first in the recent past to note the sociological neglect of women, except as wives and mothers.

CHAPTER 2

The Sociology of Conjugal Roles and the Problem of Marital Equality

There have been many attempts to describe the patterning of conjugal roles (Hammond and Oeser, 1954; Burgess, Locke and Thomes, 1963; Blood and Wolfe, 1960; Christensen, 1964). One of the most influential contributions is the work of Bott (1971), who studied twenty London families and collected data on four main areas of family life: housework, child-care, decision-making and leisure interests and activities, including contact with relatives, friends and neighbours. After trying to work with various classificatory schemes, Bott settled on the distinction between segregated conjugal role relationships and joint conjugal role relationships. The former refers to 'a relationship in which complementary and independent types of organisation predominate. Husband and wife have a clear differentiation of tasks and a considerable number of separate interests and activities. They have a clearly defined division of labour into male tasks and female tasks. They expect to have different leisure pursuits, and the husband has his friends outside the home and the wife has hers' (Bott, 1971, p. 53). In contrast, a joint conjugal role relationship refers to 'a relationship in which joint organisation is relatively predominant. Husband and wife expect to carry out many activities together with a minimum of task differentiation and separation of interests. They not only plan the affairs of the family together but also exchange many household tasks and spend much of their leisure time together' (ibid., pp. 53-4).

For the moment I am not concerned with the explanation of the patterning of conjugal roles, but with the meaning(s) attached to the concepts 'joint' and 'segregated'. Bott herself was essentially concerned with the expectations couples expressed regarding the organisation of familial activities, although role performance and an authority dimension are also alluded to on occasions.[1] More critically, although Bott found complementary, independent and joint conjugal role organisation in all the families she studied, she classified each couple in her sample according to the predominant pattern of conjugal role segregation. Subsequent research has suggested that activities tend to

be organised differently in different spheres and therefore it is doubtful whether 'jointness' or 'segregation' refer to general characteristics
of marriage (Platt, 1969; Harrell-Bond, 1969).

The problematic nature of the definition and measurement of
conjugal roles is also highlighted by the observation that studies which
rely on measures of domestic task performance produce different
results from studies which have either used data on 'socio-emotional'
activities or have followed Bott and used composite measures of
jointness (Toomey, 1971). Contradictory findings have also been
attributed to whether or not precise questions were asked about
specific tasks or more general questions about attitudes were used
(Oakley, 1974).

According to Oakley, in many conjugal role studies,[2] 'an assumption of gender role differences appears as a kind of baseline from
which questions are asked and assessments made' (ibid., pp. 161-5).
An example discussed by Oakley of a highly biased selection of questions concerns the tendency to ask more frequently about domestic
tasks that men are more likely to participate in. Secondly, an example
of the way in which bias can enter into the classification of data (again
taken from Oakley) concerns the work of Toomey. In his study of
Kent couples Toomey classed as 'joint' a husband who looked after
the children 'very often', whereas for doing the laundry the responses
'very often', 'often', 'sometimes' and 'rarely' were all classed as
'joint'. Taken together, the intrusion of gender role norms into the
selection of questions and the analysis of the answers seems likely to
result in an overgenerous estimation of the prevalence of conjugal role
'jointness'.

A related problem is the use of ambiguous criteria to determine the
degree of conjugal role segregation. In addition to the inconsistent use
of terms like 'often' and 'sometimes', it is unusual to find them
defined precisely. Consequently in the absence of any standardised
guidance to respondents, there is no way of controlling the different
meanings individual respondents attach to such vague categories.
Once again, the exact meaning of jointness is at issue. In some cases it
seems to have been used to refer to normative values rather than the
actual practice of sharing certain tasks. In other instances it refers to
the sharing of some tasks rather than others, and in still other cases it
refers to the frequent sharing of certain tasks and/or the infrequent
sharing of certain tasks. Given this bewildering range of meanings it is
clearly imperative to know exactly what 'jointness' refers to in terms
of activities and the amount of sharing necessary to qualify for the
category.

In this context the work of Turner (1967) is instructive, since his
research is regarded by Harris (1969) as the 'only satisfactory attempt

to verify Bott's hypothesis'. In his discussion of the criteria he used to distinguish degrees of conjugal role segregation, Turner noted: 'If a husband did not regularly carry out domestic duties, or if there was a rigid division of labour in respect of domestic work, the conjugal relationship was recorded as segregated.' In the case of child-rearing Turner defined as joint a couple who 'usually discussed methods of discipline and/or child-rearing' and 'shared certain of the tasks of child-rearing' (1967, p. 124). This methodology leaves unclear once again how 'rigidly', 'regularly' or 'often' an activity has to be shared to be classified as 'joint'.

To classify as joint a couple whose conjugal role behaviour involves either spouse in a disproportionate level of participation in any one or more areas of family life might be considered reasonable if it were not for the tendency to link together discussions of conjugal role jointness and marital equality. This association of the notions jointness and equality has in fact been present in the literature at least since the time of Bott. For example, in her description of a joint couple Bott includes the idea that a 'husband and wife should be equals' (1971, p. 52) and elsewhere Bott refers to 'joint organisation with its ethic of equality' (ibid., p. 83). Although Bott operates throughout with a composite measure of jointness and consequently alludes to a general notion of marital equality (ibid., p. 95), occasionally she restricts her references to equality to one aspect of the marital relationship, notably authority (ibid., p. 80).

Certainly many researchers have regarded jointness and equality as synonymous when interpreting Bott and their own data (McKinley, 1964, p. 119; Holter, 1970, p. 14; Pahl and Pahl, 1971, pp. 207-10; Oppong, 1975, pp. 803-4). However, one of the most detailed discussions of conjugal role jointness and equality is to be found in the work of Oakley (1974). Oakley also examined four areas of family life—housework, child-care, decision-making and leisure—and discussed her findings in relation to 'assertions of equality within marriage' (1974, p. 146). Oakley's analysis includes the use of two different measures of conjugal sharing which she subsequently used interchangeably. On the one hand domestic tasks and child-care activities are classified according to the husband's level of participation: namely, high, medium or low. On the other hand, decision-making and leisure are examined in terms of the distinction between segregated and joint roles. Oakley does not indicate exactly how she assessed her data, merely that all her ratings were 'relative' to the rest of the sample rather than 'absolute' (ibid., p. 137). Once again the problem with this methodology is that a relatively segregated couple in one study may be assessed as relatively joint in another. When Oakley compared her data for possible 'discrepancies', 'high' and 'medium' levels of husband participation in domestic work and child-care are clearly regarded as the equivalent of 'joint', and a 'low' level of participation in the household division of labour is correspondingly treated as the equivalent of 'segregated'.

What is perhaps the crux of Oakley's analysis is her suggestion that 'Only a minority of husbands give the kind of help that assertions of equality in modern marriage imply' (ibid., p. 138). For example, Oakley found that in housework 15 per cent of husbands participated at a 'high' level and in child-care the level was 25 per cent. In the case of decision-making and leisure, Oakley found that sharing in one sphere was associated with sharing in the other and vice versa. Thus Oakley noted that 43 per cent of her sample were characterised by a segregated conjugal role relationship in these areas of family life, although as in the case of the household division of labour, a marked social class difference was observable in the direction of a greater incidence of segregation among working-class couples.

Interpreting 'low' levels of husband participation in domestic work and child-care as evidence of conjugal role segregation, Oakley shows that this is the majority pattern among her sample in domestic tasks (60 per cent) and only just a minority pattern in child-care activities (45 per cent) and decision-making/leisure (43 per cent). Oakley concludes this part of her study by noting that today 'marriages may be characterised by an equality of status and "mutuality" between husband and wife, but inequality on the domestic task level is not automatically banished' (ibid., p. 146). Hence Oakley emphasises that even in marriages that are 'egalitarian' with respect to leisure and decision-making, 'a large pocket of domestic oppression' may also be present (ibid., p. 149).

In addition to presenting material on conjugal role behaviour, Oakley also examined attitudes and beliefs about male and female roles. She found considerable evidence for the view that primary responsibility for the home and children rested with the woman and that 'Even in joint role marriages where a man's level of participation in domestic affairs is high, a dimension of one-sided responsibility persists' (ibid., p. 159). Thus, the lack of an 'equal allocation of responsibilities' as well as a lack of extensive task-sharing in most marriages leads Oakley to be very sceptical of the view that marriage is a 'joint' or 'equal' partnership (ibid., p. 160).

In the Pahls' study of managers and their wives, marital equality is a key theme in the chapter on marriage but is left undefined. The authors tend to link egalitarianism with conjugal role jointness and imply that marital equality refers to task-sharing in all areas of family life and a sense of emotional closeness. On the basis of what appears to be exceedingly thin evidence, they report that their couples 'felt that their marital relationship was more egalitarian' compared to their parents' marriages (1971, p. 210). However they also report that 'on the whole' household tasks and decision-making were not 'shared equally' (ibid., p. 213). In their conclusions, the Pahls seem to be suggesting that their research couples had more egalitarian marriages in terms of 'closeness', but that the wives were the 'less powerful' partners whose roles were 'dependent on and determined by their husbands' (ibid., p. 236).

In a study of middle-class couples in Edinburgh, the term marital partnership was preferred and defined in terms of mutual emotional support, shared responsibility for domestic and child-care tasks, joint leisure and egalitarian decision-making (Robertson, 1975). Unfortunately, the last-mentioned feature of a partnership marriage seems to have been less fully investigated than the others. However, Robertson's research does convincingly demonstrate a low level of husband participation in the household division of labour and in this respect confirms the findings of this and Oakley's study. It also confirms the impression that certain studies tend to exaggerate the extent of conjugal role 'jointness'.

In contrast, Young and Willmott are generally much more optimistic about the decline of conjugal role segregation and the growth of marital equality (1973, p. 32). This is notwithstanding the exceedingly limited nature of some of their data (Oakley, 1974, p. 164) and their various comments to the contrary.

> Power has not been distributed equally in more than a few families. Division of labour is still the rule, with the husband doing the 'man's' work, and the wife taking prime responsibility for the housekeeping and the children.   (Young and Willmott, 1973, p. 31)

> And if contraception and more tolerant husbands enable wives to go out to work, they can win for themselves a measure of financial independence.   (ibid., p. 100)

> The wife's burden depends upon how much of it the husband will share. The seesaw can only tilt back if there is someone at the other end; and sometimes he seems to leave her on the ground.
>   (ibid., p. 277)

In the debate in the American literature on marital equality there are those (like Oakley in Britain) who have concluded that it is a 'myth' (Gillespie, 1971) and that 'there is no research proof that egalitarianism has been increasing' (Bernard, 1973). There are also those who, like Young and Willmott, insist, often in apparent contrast to their own evidence, that modern marriages are egalitarian. For example, Blood and Wolfe found that 'The typical pattern in Detroit is to make only half the decisions unilaterally (compared to three-fourths of the tasks)' (1960, p. 53). Yet the authors still claimed that the division of labour and decision-making 'are equalitarian in the sense that both husbands and wives participate' (loc. cit.). In the case of this particular study, the material on marital equality has been the subject of a major critique which suggested that Blood and Wolfe systematically exaggerate its extent (Gillespie, 1971).

One of the problems of comparing these apparently conflicting studies is that different researchers are using the term 'equality' to refer to different things. For instance, Bott's brief allusions to marital equality mainly concern norms, not behaviour. In the light of the trend towards greater sexual equality in society,[3] it may well be that egalitarian norms are easier to elicit than evidence of egalitarian behaviour. All the other studies mentioned in this context are essentially concerned with marital behaviour, although the specific sphere(s) of activity varies. For example, Oakley, Young and Willmott, and Blood and Wolfe all refer to domestic, leisure and decision-making data in their discussions of marital equality, whereas Gillespie and Bernard concentrate on the distribution of marital power and authority.

Following from this issue, a further problem concerns the pattern of behaviour in any one or more areas of family life that is to count as egalitarian. There are, in fact, two aspects to this problem: one relates to what activities are included in any assessment of marital equality and the other relates to how they are judged. For example, regarding the first aspect, Oakley only inquired about the following household tasks: cleaning, shopping, cooking, washing, washing-up and ironing (1974, p. 214). Bott (1971, p. 233) and Blood and Wolfe (1960, p. 282), on the other hand, used a far less restrictive notion of 'housework' that included household repairs, gardening and decorating. Thus in the same way that Oakley has criticised the androcentric bias of certain (male) sociologists (1976, p. 182), she in turn is open to the opposite criticism, namely, that she operates with a gynecocentric definition of what constitutes housework. Young and Willmott tend to avoid this particular problem by defining such things as home-decorating and repairs as leisure activities, although many of their male respondents certainly did not share this opinion (1973, p. 209).

Interestingly, since only one of Oakley's sample of married women with at least one child under 5 worked full-time outside the home, it should come as no surprise to find that most of the husbands scored low on domestic and child-care participation. In other words, it could be argued that, given the limited range of tasks included under the heading of housework, plus the husband's greater unavailability owing to his primary responsibility for breadwinning, such a finding was virtually assured. Whether or not it is justifiable to conclude from this that marital equality is lacking in most families is questionable. It may well be that the husbands who performed only a token amount of domestic work in Oakley's terms were busy painting, decorating, building shelves, gardening, and so on. The logic of Oakley's analysis would seem to be that in order to achieve marital equality a husband should return from work and play a major part in certain household tasks such as washing and cleaning. The object of Oakley's indignation regarding the myth of marital equality should be the prevailing highly differentiated sexual division of labour and not the patterning of conjugal behaviour that is predicated upon such a division of labour. Thus, Oakley's notion of marital equality seems to exclude the possibility of spouses making different yet equal contributions to the household. In this respect, Oakley's work is similar to Bott's, who also only included activities that were undertaken by the husband and wife together or at different times in her category of 'joint' (1971, p. 53). Alternatively, Blood and Wolfe's notion of marital equality encompasses the pattern whereby activities and decisions are made together and the pattern in which an equal number of separate activities and decisions are carried out independently by each spouse.

The analysis so far suggests that one of the central issues in the debate about the prevalence of conjugal role jointness/equality concerns one's operational definitions. The crucial links between concepts, the scales used to measure them and one's findings, can be well illustrated with the data collected in this study on reported conjugal role behaviour in the household division of labour. Table 2.1 compares the results of using two contrasting operational definitions of conjugal role jointness. The data refer to the incidence of conjugal

Table 2.1 *The Incidence of Conjugal Role Jointness and Segregation Using Two Methods of Analysis*

Task area	Method 1 (Unequal jointness)				Method 2 (Equal jointness)			
	Joint		Segregated		Joint		Segregated	
	No.	(%)	No.	(%)	No.	(%)	No.	(%)
Domestic	26	(69)	12	(31)	0	(0)	38	(100)
Child-care	36	(95)	2	(5)	17	(45)	21	(55)

role jointness among the research couples in domestic and child-care tasks. In Method 1 the responses 'husbands only' and 'wife only' were classified as 'segregated' and the responses 'husbands mostly', 'wife mostly', and 'husband and wife equally' were classified as 'joint'. For the second method the response 'husband and wife equally' was alone used to refer to conjugal role jointness and all unequal combinations of spouse participation were classified as segregated.

Not surprisingly, the two different methods of calculating conjugal role jointness and segregation show that the first method produces a far greater apparent incidence of conjugal role jointness than the second method in both parts of the household division of labour. Hence the same data can be used to support quite divergent conclusions. For example, when 'jointness' is defined imprecisely as any degree of sharing, however minimal, it becomes possible to interpret token male domesticity within marriage as evidence of conjugal role jointness. If subsequently it is implied that jointness is indicative of marital equality, then one has achieved the impression that marital jointness/equality is indeed widespread. Alternatively, by using the 'equal jointness' method, it is possible to show that few couples are characterised by jointness in the household division of labour and to conclude that marital jointness/equality is virtually non-existent. At the very least this exercise suggests that when husbands are primarily responsible for financial provision and wives for the home and children, it is most unlikely that they will participate equally in the household division of labour. If anything less than equal spouse participation in domestic and child-care tasks is used as evidence for 'jointness' and 'equality', then most couples can be shown to participate in certain activities some of the time, however infrequently. Consequently to imply that jointness and equality are synonymous in some way can often lead to misleading and/or contradictory conclusions. Consideration of the prevailing sexual division of labour strongly suggests that in the interests of clarity, the notion of equality should be restricted to the analysis of marital power and authority, and that the notion of jointness should be treated as one (relatively low) degree of conjugal role segregation. This is basically the approach adopted by Bott (1971, p. 55). However, the use of a composite measure of the degree of segregation of conjugal roles, plus the use of the term 'equality' in conjunction with her discussions of conjugal role jointness, introduced a considerable amount of ambiguity into this central aspect of her study.[4]

Assuming for the moment that a lack of conjugal role segregation is indicative of marital equality as Oakley (1974) and others suggest, the above analysis, like that of Oakley, remains vulnerable to the criticism that it involves a particular and limited notion of marital equality, namely, the equal sharing of the same tasks by husbands and wives. The work of Blood and Wolfe (1960) suggests that the equal sharing of different tasks represents a plausible alternative meaning to the concept of marital equality. Certainly the research couples in this study, and I suspect in other studies too, operated with this 'different but equal' notion of marital equality in the process of judging what was, and what was not, 'fair' in their marriages. Moreover, the apparently straightforward allocation of tasks to each spouse on a strictly numerical basis ignores the possibility that a qualitative differentiation of tasks may also be relevant. The 'who does what' trade-off within marriage clearly varies and constitutes a strong argument against the imposition of an 'objective' measure of marital equality with reference to husband and wife participation and specialisation in the household division of labour. These and other problems that relate to the identification of marital equality are illustrated below with the aid of case-study data collected from professional workers and their wives at the child-rearing stage of the family life-cycle.

Case 1

Mr and Mrs Holden were in their late twenties and had one child under a year at the time of the fieldwork. They had recently moved to the north when Mr Holden joined his present employer as an industrial scientist. Mrs Holden was a full-time mother and housewife. Within the context of their primary role responsibilities, there was little task specialisation in the Holdens' marriage. Mrs Holden undertook the bulk of the housework and child-rearing but when Mr Holden returned from work, these activities, especially the former, were mainly shared. Mr Holden was solely responsible for the 'family' car and took the major responsibility for house repairs. Mrs Holden always chose the child's clothes and saw to the laundry but all other domestic and child-care tasks, plus gardening, decorating, decision-making and leisure activities were shared to a greater or lesser extent subject to the couple's availability. On a simple numerical basis, the Holdens' pattern of conjugal behaviour could be said to be predominantly segregated with respect to the household division of labour and predominantly 'joint' with respect to decision-making and leisure. However, in certain respects such a description is misleading since the basic sex role structure of the Holdens' situation precluded Mr Holden from participating in a major way in the household division of labour. Yet, the inclusion of 'traditional male' as well as 'traditional female' tasks in one's definition of domestic work (in the context of the Holdens' primary sex role responsibilities) suggests that the extent of conjugal role 'jointness' in this case is considerable. In other words, if one operates with a notional eight-hour working day, then the Holdens' 'after-hours' conjugal pattern could be said to be highly 'joint' with respect to their household division of labour. Such a pattern could also be judged to be egalitarian in the sense that beyond their specialised role responsibilities that might fairly be regarded as complementary and equal, Mr and Mrs Holden shared in a 'joint' and equal manner most other family tasks and activities. As far as decision-making and leisure are concerned, a more detailed analysis suggests that whilst these spheres are superficially 'joint' and equal, in other respects they are less than egalitarian, as the subsequent chapters on these topics will reveal.

Case 2

Mr and Mrs Price were both nearly 50 years old and had two adult children who both lived at home. Mr Price was an industrial scientist and Mrs Price had been a full-time mother and housewife since she left work to have her first child. In terms of domestic and child-care tasks, the Prices had a markedly segregated conjugal role relationship. Mrs Price did all the shopping and the laundry and the vast bulk of the cooking and cleaning. Mr Price did all the budgeting, house and car maintenance and most of the gardening. The Prices reported that a majority of their leisure time and decision-making was shared, although, as noted above, a more detailed examination of these spheres will be presented later. Thus Mr and Mrs Price had a distinctly segregated household division of labour in which Mr Price's level of participation in activities that are conventionally described as 'female tasks' was extremely low by any standards. Similarly, Mrs Price's level of participation in activities that are conventionally regarded as 'masculine tasks' was also small. However, although their respective contributions were quite different, it could still be argued that they were making equal contributions. Mr Price seemed to compensate for his lack of 'domesticity' in certain areas of family life by being particularly active in home decoration, repairs and general improvements. Moreover, although Mrs Price was almost solely responsible for a whole range of domestic and child-care tasks, she also enjoyed considerably more leisure time than her breadwinning husband. Consequently, in this marriage, the working day and 'after-hours' conjugal pattern was highly segregated, yet none the less could be regarded as essentially egalitarian.

Case 3

Mr and Mrs Jarvis were both in their early forties and had two adolescent children. They both worked full-time outside the home, Mr Jarvis as an industrial scientist, and his wife as a teacher. Mr and Mrs Jarvis reported that they both participated in child-care tasks to an equal extent but that their domestic task pattern involved considerable segregation. The husband took major but not sole responsibility for the maintenance of the house and car whilst Mrs Jarvis was mainly responsible for cooking, cleaning, washing and shopping. With two incomes, Mr and Mrs Jarvis were able to pay others to repair the house and car and clean the house, activities that had previously been undertaken by themselves. Mr Jarvis tended to work longer hours than his wife and correspondingly tended to do less in the home, although since his wife had returned to full-time work outside the home his level of participation in the household division of labour had increased, especially in child-care tasks. Leisure activities, including gardening, and decision-making were reported as predominantly 'joint' and equal activities. Mr and Mrs Jarvis represent a good example of a 'symmetrical family' in the Young and Willmott (1973) sense. They both worked outside and inside the home; Mr Jarvis was the major breadwinner in the family and played a relatively minor role in the domestic work; Mrs Jarvis was also a breadwinner and played a major part in the domestic sphere. Therefore, although Mr and Mrs Jarvis conformed to a symmetrical variant of marital equality, an element of conjugal role segregation on the basis of sex persisted in their marriage.

Thus, several different meanings may be attached to the term marital equality and there would seem to be no straightforward and objectively identifiable single pattern that alone merits the label marital equality. Basically, if domestic work is considered as work comparable in a contributory sense to paid work outside the home, it is conceivable that a couple can make similar yet equal contributions, dissimilar yet equal contributions, or be characterised by a combination of both variations. Furthermore, it is also quite possible for a couple to be equal in one sphere of their marriage and highly unequal in other respects. Consequently, Platt's reservations regarding 'the unidimensionality of jointness/segregation of conjugal roles' (1969, p. 295) would seem to apply to the issue of marital equality/inequality.

The problem of what to include and exclude in one's study of marital equality has been shown to be crucial and highly susceptible to bias, notably in terms of gender. For instance, to avoid implying that a lack of male domesticity in relation to certain 'feminine' household tasks precludes the attainment of marital equality (Oakley, 1974, p. 164), the prevailing sexual division of labour should be taken into account, including the tendency for husbands to be the major breadwinners and the tendency for wives to participate in only a small way in certain 'masculine' household tasks. Moreover, in an effort to clarify some of the conflicting evidence and conclusions in this area of research, the fundamental importance of measurement in relation to definitional problems has been highlighted. And as one moves from a purely quantitative to a more qualitative analysis in an attempt to draw up some kind of balance-sheet of a couple's respective contributions, the difficulty and/or significance attached to various activities has also been shown to be relevant. It may well be that conventional definitions of 'work' in the context of different family roles and the extent to which such notions intrude into one's idea of what constitutes marital equality underpin certain studies and the interpretation of research findings. For example, if a spouse spends an inordinate amount of time preparing meals or redecorating the house, should such activities be regarded as leisure or housework and how do they rate in terms of the problem of estimating the incidence of marital equality? Who does what and how it is valued is clearly dependent upon the underlying distribution of power and which spouse, if any, has most say in the allocation of tasks and their evaluation.

In the light of all these problems, and above all the difficulty of selecting one notion of marital equality among many competing notions in a non-arbitrary manner, there would seem to be a strong case for distinguishing between the degree of conjugal role segregation in the household division of labour, and marital equality, and restricting the latter to consideration of conjugal power and authority. The main point is that conjugal role segregation is not necessarily inconsistent with the idea of marital equality and that conjugal role jointness is not necessarily the same thing as marital equality. This is not to deny that the distribution of marital power can be both a cause and effect of the nature and extent of conjugal role segregation. Rather, it is to suggest that segregation should not be confused with marital equality. Finally, an understanding of the patterning of conjugal role relationships would not seem to be possible in isolation from an analysis of the prevailing sexual division of labour.

Notes: Chapter 2

1 See especially Chapter 3.
2 Notably Bott (1971), Platt (1969), Toomey (1971) and Young and Willmott (1973).
3 Summaries of the extent of the achievement of female emancipation in legal, political, economic and social terms with reference to Britain and elsewhere can be found in Gavron (1966), Goode (1970) and Wainwright (1978). For an account of the impact of recent equality of the sexes legislation in Britain on the position of women, see Coussins (1977).
4 Bott's analysis of social networks has also been criticised for its lack of conceptual clarity (Turner, 1967; Harris, 1969).

CHAPTER 3

Social Theory and the Sexual Division of Labour

In the sociological study of the family, it is widely accepted that in contemporary industrial capitalist societies there is a marked sexual division of labour in society and the family. For example, Goode, drawing heavily on the work of Parsons (1956) and his research associates, has stated (1964, p. 71):

> The parallel between jobs and the major role obligations is clear. The mother begins with the nurturance of the child, establishing a close physical and psychological bond because of the gratifications both give to one another. Her social relational tasks are expressive, emotional and integrative. She is to console, to nurse, to bring together again those who have quarrelled. The father is the instrumental leader, organising the family for production, political conflicts or war. He must solve the problem of the outside environment, social or physical . . . this allocation of tasks exists in most societies.

Harris makes the same point in a less Parsonian manner (1969, pp. 124-5).

> In the first place there are obvious advantages in a sexual division of labour within the family: that is to say in one partner specialising in child-rearing and household management and the other in providing the material means of support. Except where the earnings of the husband are high or the wife's potential earnings through employment outside the family are high, it will not be possible to employ someone to take over the child-rearing and household management tasks. Since the wife must be periodically absent from employment through child-bearing she is the obvious candidate for the family-oriented role.

Harris goes on to qualify this statement, implying that he does not regard it as an entirely satisfactory explanation of the current sexual division of labour. For instance, he notes that this argument does not apply with equal force at all stages of the family cycle, and elsewhere he notes that there would seem to be no biological grounds for ascribing a family-oriented role to women. Consequently, since there would seem to be very few tasks either inside or outside the family, apart from the bearing of children, that cannot be accomplished in modern society by either men or women (Goffman, 1977), the sexual divisions that actually exist cannot be wholly or partially attributed to the 'biological peculiarities of the two sexes' (Goode, 1964, p. 70).

In fact most social theories do not dissent from this view. The one notable exception is the functionalist theory of the family developed by Parsons. Due to industrialisation, suggests Parsons, 'The type of occupational structure which is so essential to our society requires a far reaching structural segregation of occupational roles from kinship roles of the same individuals' (1964, pp. 191-2). This segregation takes two forms. Individual conjugal families become structurally isolated from wider kin. Within a conjugal family, sex role differentiation becomes the norm, in the form of husbands being accorded major responsibility for the occupationally based 'instrumental leadership role', and wives the major responsibility for the family-based 'expressive leadership role'. The reasons for this pattern of role differentiation concern the functional exigencies of the occupational and family systems in modern societies, both systems performing vital functions for society. The problem according to Parsons is that the occupational values of achievement, universalism, impersonality and specificity potentially conflict with the kinship values of ascription, particularism, affectivity and diffuseness. In order for both systems to coexist and function effectively, it is necessary to separate their operations as far as possible. The efficiency of the occupational system needs to be 'unhampered by "personal" considerations', 'requires' mobility, and must prevent occupational competition between spouses that could threaten the harmony and solidarity of the family. Conversely, the family system needs to be highly solidaristic, 'especially in relation to the socialisation of individuals'. Thus, Parsons's functional analysis of the structural interdependence of two fundamental institutional spheres of society indicates that the segregation of conjugal families from kin, and the segregation of male roles from female roles, is the only arrangement that 'interferes least with the functional needs of the occupational system' (ibid., p. 192), and one which 'is probably the least exposed to strain' (ibid., p. 79).

However, this necessarily universal and inevitable structural form is not without its exceptions or problems. First, Parsons notes that the development of the relatively isolated conjugal family 'is uneven and important tendencies to deviation from it are found', notably among rural, elite, and lower-class rural and urban families (ibid., p. 185). This aspect of Parsons's theory has been the subject of considerable research and critical discussion, the main thrust of which casts severe doubts on the validity of the isolated family generalisation and links this issue to the wider debate concerning the role of kinship in modern society and the transfer of functions from family to non-family institutions (Harris, 1969; Goode, 1970; Morgan, 1975).

Of more immediate relevance is the problematic nature of the functional necessity for sex role differentiation within any one, relatively isolated, conjugal family. Parsons himself is not unaware of the possible contradiction between the 'paramount value system' of egalitarianism, and sex role inequality. As a result of the functional necessity of 'confining the number of status-giving occupational roles of members of the effective conjugal unit to one', a 'typically asymmetrical relation of the marriage pair to the occupational structure' is produced (Parsons, 1964, pp. 191, 192). Thus it is 'inherent' in the situation that:

> The separation of the sex roles in our society is such as, for the most part, to remove women from the kind of occupational status which is so important for the determination of the status of the family.　(ibid., p. 80)

> The normal married woman is debarred from testing or demonstrating her fundamental equality with her husband in competitive occupational achievement.　(ibid., p. 193)

Finally, according to Parsons there is a 'general' tendency 'to "shunt" the feminine role out of primary status in the occupational system or competition for occupational success or status' (ibid., p. 423). In sum, it is 'obvious' to Parsons that the relative exclusion of women 'from some of the highest prestige statuses', and as a consequence their relegation 'to a narrower range of functions than men', represents a 'fundamental limitation on full "equality of opportunity"' (ibid., p. 423).[1]

In contrast to this marked lack of sexual equality in occupational terms, it is 'reassuring' to be told that 'there is still an element of status which they share equally' (ibid., p. 77). This is within marriage: 'in their capacity of husband and wife, it is very important that they should be treated as equals' (ibid., p. 79). As if to compensate for a lack of occupational equality between spouses, Parsons emphasises elsewhere that 'they must be evaluated in certain respects as equals' (ibid., p. 422).

Parsons's theory therefore concedes sex role inequality as 'normal' in the occupational system whilst propagating the idea that within marriage the roles of men and women are different but equal. One of the major difficulties with this analysis is that the acquisition of equality through marriage is in no way guaranteed, precisely because of the widespread tendency for husbands to be primarily responsible for the economic support of the conjugal family. Moreover, the ramifications of the relative exclusion of married women from occupational life extend, I would suggest, far beyond the crucial fact of the wife's economic dependency and therefore subordination.[2] At one point Parsons seems to recognise the weakness of his case when he suggests the lack of occupational equality 'creates a demand for a functional equivalent' (ibid., p. 193)—an exercise which, in the urban middle classes (Parsons's main concern), leads to the rejection of the housewife role on the grounds that it involves 'menial functions', and an emphasis on humanistic values as expressed in 'personal appearance, house furnishings, cultural things like literature and music' (ibid., p. 194). However, this vicarious, non-utilitarian style of life does not overcome the dependent economic and social status of the vast majority of housewives, and may even exacerbate it. Thus Veblen pointed out as long ago as 1899 that the middle-class housewife 'still quite unmistakenly remains his chattel in theory; for the habitual rendering of vicarious leisure and consumption is the abiding mark of the unfree servant' (Veblen, 1970, p. 69).

A related source of criticism that strikes at the foundation of Parsons's analysis concerns his distinction between instrumental and expressive leadership roles. Parsons claims that, due to the functional exigencies of the occupational and family systems, the husband alone 'must be accorded the "instrumental leadership" role' and the wife the 'expressive leadership' role (1964, pp. 422-3). Such a differentiation of roles is characteristic of all small groups, says Parsons, and in another publication he elaborates his biological and social explanation of the need to allocate role responsibilities by sex (1956, pp. 23-4):

> The bearing and early nursing of children establish a strong presumptive primacy of the relation of mother to small child and this in turn establishes a presumption that the man, who is exempted from these biological functions, should specialise in the alternative direction . . .
>
> It is our suggestion that the recent change in the American family itself and in its relation to the rest of society which we have taken as our point of departure, is far from implying an erasure of the differentiation of sex roles; in many respects it reinforces and clarifies it. In the first place, the articulation between family and occupational system in our society focuses the instrumental

responsibility for a family very sharply on its one adult male member, and prevents its diffusion through the ramifications of an extended kinship system. Secondly, the isolation of the nuclear family in a complementary way focuses the responsibility of the mother role more sharply on the one adult woman, to a relatively high degree cutting her off from the help of adult sisters and other kinswomen: furthermore the fact of the absence of the husband-father from the home premises so much of the time means that she has to take the primary responsibility for the children. This responsibility is partly mitigated by reduction in the number of children and by aids to household management, but by no means to the point of emancipating the mother from it.

In support of his view that there is a universal tendency for family roles to become specialised in either an instrumental or an expressive manner and to be allocated according to sex, Parsons draws upon Freudian theory, experimental research with small groups and cross-cultural data. For many reasons each of these sources of validation is suspect. For example, Freudian theory has been likened to religion and art on the grounds that it is 'essentially non-scientific and to be judged in terms of belief and faith rather than in terms of proof and verification' (Eysenck, 1962, p. 226). In the case of the small group research undertaken by Bales and others, it can be forcefully argued that findings derived from transitory experimental groups of male students are not especially applicable to a developing structure of intimate relationships that is typically characterised by the presence of individuals of different ages and sexes (Morgan, 1975). Similarly, the cross-cultural research quoted by Parsons is also of doubtful relevance due mainly to the unreliability of the original studies and the methods used to evaluate them. For instance, Zelditch himself admits that he sacrificed 'both a great deal of information and the more refined aspects of analysis, for a simple replication of cases' (Parsons, 1956, p. 315); that he 'accepted as accurate' all ethnographic reports and that 'the character of the indices used was determined by fortuitous circumstances' (Parsons, 1956, p. 317). However, the methodological inadequacies of this material do not seem to have had a cautionary effect on Parsons's theorising.

In addition to the methodological limitations of the supporting evidence for his theories, Parsons's basic conceptual distinction between instrumental and expressive activities/functions has also been the subject of considerable criticism. For example, in a comparative study using data from America and Greece it was concluded that these types of activities 'are not clearly and neatly distributed to men and women in the expected correspondence' (Safilios-Rothschild, 1969,

p. 301). More fundamentally, Morgan has questioned the meaning and validity of the distinction and has suggested that one person may perform both types of activities and that some activities may involve a combination of expressive and instrumental elements (1975, pp. 44-5).

Another recent critic, Oakley, is particularly severe on Parsons. She suggests that his theory of sex role differentiation 'appears logical but is actually erroneous' (1976, p. 179). This is because it is only Parsons's androcentric bias that leads him to presume that biology establishes primacy and then to consider it necessary in the family and society for roles to be allocated consistently by sex. However, whilst feminists such as Oakley rightly object to pseudo-scientific theories that ascribe women's role to be dominated by the home and children, it should also be noted that such theories also ascribe men's place to be outside the home, albeit in a role that confers greater power and status. In practice, a major weakness of Parsons's universal necessity for sex role differentiation is indicated by the fact that not all men and women conform strictly to the functionalist model. For example, many women choose not to bear children, others have a 'career', and often husbands are unemployed.

To continue in this more practical vein, in contrast to the highly abstract, vague and essentially cultural description of sex roles provided by Parsons, if consideration is given to the content of such roles, the questionable distinction between instrumental and expressive roles is revealed. In the typically small modern conjugal family, the wife-mother role is far from expressive. It is more accurately domestic work. Tasks such as cleaning, washing, ironing, and so on, are, it could be argued, neither expressive nor instrumental in the Parsonian sense of the terms. Although Parsons suggests that 'homemaking' is an 'internal instrumental responsibility' that the wife-mother combines with her expressive role (1964, p. 423), it is difficult to reconcile this formulation with Parsons's definition of an instrumental function, namely, one that involves the establishment of 'desired relations to *external* goal-objects' (1956, p. 47). Occupational roles are equally difficult to designate unequivocally in terms of this distinction, since many involve both instrumental and expressive elements. Thus family and occupational roles would not seem to be easily or usefully identified by these concepts. Moreover, in cases where there is a clear differentiation of functions, there would seem to be few reasons for, and little advantage in, restricting role allocation and performance according to sex. The theoretical and practical possibility that both instrumental and expressive functions can be performed by one person, or the possibility of a less specialised and more flexible conjugal arrangement, are dismissed by Parsons without serious consideration.

Finally, the instrumental male role and the expressive female role are of such great 'functional significance' to the stability and effectiveness of the family and society that couples with sufficient economic resources (that is, the most 'successful' members of society) consistently absent themselves from an achieved occupational role and employ others to care for their children and perform domestic tasks.

Consequently, the assertions made by Goode (1964) and Harris (1969) regarding the lack of inevitability of sex role differentiation would not seem to be seriously threatened by the exception of Parsons's functionalist theory. On the contrary, it is difficult not to conclude that in the case of Parsons, 'the total impact of the work is to provide a justification for the prevailing family and economic system' (Morgan, 1975, p. 43)—a system that undoubtedly involves considerable sexual differentiation, or sexual inequality, depending upon one's viewpoint.

However, the lack of support for Parsons's theory of sex roles does not seem to have diminished his influence among certain sociologists. Acceptance and approval of the 'normality' of a full-time home role for a wife and a full-time work role outside the home for a husband is often indicated in sociological studies. This is most marked in those very societies in which, due to the reduction of the physical component in many occupational roles, the widespread use of birth control and the availability of alternatives to breast feeding, the need for sex role ascription is arguably less and less defensible. One such sociologist is Bott, who in her introduction to the key chapter on conjugal roles and social networks wrote: 'in all families there was a basic division of labour, by which the husband was primarily responsible for supporting the family financially and the wife was responsible for housework and child-care . . . But within this general division of labour, there was considerable variation of detail' (1971, p. 54). Bott agrees with Parsons that a 'basic division of labour between husband and wife' is of 'fundamental importance' (ibid., p. 81) and she seems to regard it as entirely non-problematic in terms of the patterning of conjugal roles. In fact the general Parsonian character of Bott's work is thinly veiled but does not seem to be widely appreciated.[3] Both are concerned with the implications of the increasing structural isolation of couples due to social and geographical mobility: Parsons with reference to kinship, sex roles and socialisation, and Bott with reference to conjugal role relationships. According to Parsons, 'spouses are thrown upon each other' by virtue of their 'structurally unsupported' situation in which 'Neither party has any other adult kin on whom they have a right to "lean for support" ' (1956, pp. 19-20). For Bott, in loose-knit social networks, a couple's 'external relationships are relatively discontinuous both in space and time'. Consequently, 'In facing the external world they draw on each other ... Hence their high standards of conjugal compatibility, their stress on shared interests, on joint organisation, on equality between husband and wife. They must get along well together, they must help one another in carrying out familial tasks, for there is no sure external source of material and emotional help' (1971, p. 95).

In more general terms, both Parsons and Bott are advancing the view that one cannot separate an analysis of internal family relationships (Parsons emphasises parental roles and Bott conjugal roles) from an appreciation of the external social environment. Parsons's tendency to assume, on the basis of little evidence at the time, that all families are isolated, has merely been qualified by Bott with special reference to the relationship between variations in the extent to which couples are isolated and their degree of conjugal role segregation. Thus, Bott's work can be seen as a logical extension of Parsons's theory of the relative structural isolation of the individual conjugal family and in certain respects is therefore susceptible to many of the criticisms that have been directed at Parsons in this and other publications, particularly his treatment of sex roles (Morgan, 1975; Oakley, 1976).

An approach which takes directly into account the possible significance of the sexual division of labour for marriage is Turner's book on family interaction (1970). He fully recognises that 'the critical anchorage of the characteristic male role is to his occupation or career' and that 'other major institutional anchorages for the adult male role tend to be overshadowed by the occupational base' (p. 255). Turner proceeds to argue that in modern society it is practically impossible to be a 'man' without an occupation (loc. cit.).

> ... a man is adjudged prima facie to have performed a major share of his responsibilities as husband and father just by virtue of having a good record in the world of work, and it is only with great effort that we are able to think of a man as a good husband and father unless he takes his work responsibilities seriously.

Conversely, a woman's role in modern society 'has been defined as a complement to the male role, its content determined by which tasks were not assumed by men and its standing subordinate' (ibid., p. 266). Thus the woman's role, unlike the man's, does not involve the assumption of an occupation. Instead it involves two components: mother and housewife.

Whatever the historical sources of the separation between husband as breadwinner and wife as homemaker (Zaretsky, 1976), there is no doubt that this arrangement is thoroughly embedded in the social structure. Despite various pieces of legislation designed to equalise the economic position of men and women in society, there is considerable evidence that women's role in society has not changed dramatically as a result (Mackie and Pattullo, 1977). First, for example, it can be shown that in 1961, over forty years after the Sex Disqualification (Removal) Act, 1919, which made it illegal to discriminate against women entering the professions, only 15.9 per cent of doctors, 13.8 per cent of accountants, 12.5 per cent of university teachers, 6.8 per cent of dentists, 3.5 per cent of judges, barristers, advocates and solicitors, and 2.3 per cent of surveyors and architects were women (Myrdal and Klein, 1968, p. 58). Moreover, the situation does not seem to have improved since 1961 despite the expansion of higher education and professional occupations (Central Statistical Office, 1974; Wainwright, 1978). Secondly, the more recent and much vaunted Equal Pay Act and sex discrimination legislation of 1970 and 1975 have not markedly reduced the gap between the earnings of men and women (Equal Opportunities Commission, 1978a), partly because of the continued influence of past discriminatory practices (Nandy and Nandy, 1975). Consequently, 'The latest figures show that women's average hourly earnings now stand at 75.5 per cent of men's. The gap has closed slightly since 1970, but it is still substantial and progress in this respect has slowed down in the last year. In practice, the earnings gap is even greater than these figures indicate because the latter exclude the effects of overtime. In money terms the gap has actually widened' (Equal Opportunities Commission, 1978a, p. 78). Thirdly, taxation and social policy discriminate against women mainly on the basis of the assumption that men are the heads of households and consequently it is the responsibility of husbands to support their wives (Land, 1976; Wainwright, 1978). For example, in the case of single-parent families, the official expectation is that lone fathers 'are required to register for work and take any available job which is suitable' (Finer, 1974, p. 338), whereas a lone mother can decide for herself 'whether the family will benefit more from her presence at home or from the earnings she could get from full-time work' (loc. cit.). The report stated that 'this policy is based partly on the view, which the [Supplementary Benefits] Commission believe still to be generally held, that it is usually better for children to look to a father who conforms to the normal role of breadwinner'.

Given the degree to which the husband-breadwinner, wife-homemaker roles are institutionalised, it is no surprise to find that, in the strategic cases of dual-career couples and unemployed husbands, the primary responsibility for the home and children tends to be retained by the wife (Rapoport and Rapoport, 1971; Marsden and Duff, 1975). In modern society at least, earning a living and supporting a family is equated with masculinity (Holter, 1970). Consequently the loss of work by a husband involves a loss of masculine status that an increased participation in (female) housework does less than nothing to prevent (Marsden and Duff, 1975, pp. 163-75).

The majority of the sample in the present and other similar studies have expectations that are entirely congruent with this pattern of sex role behaviour. The crucially important point about the extensive institutionalisation of such values is that the whole structure and its attendant expectations have consequences for the patterning of conjugal role relationships. Turner (1970) has drawn particular attention to some of the features of the husband's work role that have implications in this direction. First of all the meaning of work has already been alluded to with reference to the notion of masculinity. Here it is necessary to expand the point by noting that studies of male unemployment and retirement indicate that a man's occupation is likely to be his major source of identity (Jahoda, Lazarsfeld and Zeisel, 1972; Tunstall, 1966; Rosow, 1967). Such studies highlight the loss of morale, prestige, and above all identity following redundancy or retirement. In the case of professional workers, identification with work is likely to take a highly positive and intrinsic form, as is indicated by the use of the terms 'calling' (Weber, 1976; Greenwood, 1957) and 'vocation' (Weber, 1964; Gross, 1958) in such contexts.

A related but analytically distinct aspect of the meaning of work concerns its importance as a source of income and power (Morse and Weiss, 1955). This is a source which not only accrues to the husband but which is usually greater than any other source. Partly as a result of the identity, prestige, income and power conferring nature of the male breadwinning role, the demands of the husband's occupation are typically regarded as pre-eminent in a family. Turner has expressed this important point well (1970, p. 257):

... work life makes demands on time and energy that are granted legitimate priority over demands from other institutional spheres. That a man's job requires him to work late or be out of town on a business trip is sufficient excuse for declining or cancelling almost any other form of engagement. Job transfer or an opportunity to better himself professionally is sufficient justification for leaving friends, disrupting children's schooling, and abandoning community responsibilities to move the household to another community. The schedule determined by work determines the life schedule and the schedule into which other relationships must fit. The work schedule may relent occasionally to take account of illness or exceptional demands of sentiment, but ordinarily all other aspects of the life schedule must accommodate to the work schedule, even to the extent of the number of days that one may be ill.

The ramifications of a husband's work role, with special reference to the character of certain professional occupations, for conjugal role relationships will be explored in subsequent chapters. For the moment it is necessary to note that the analysis of occupational influences on family life is not an especially new topic (Edgell, 1970), although it is possibly not a widely researched one. However, there exist several pieces of research that testify to the validity of approaching conjugal roles from the standpoint of the occupational base of the husband's breadwinning role. The general subordination of family life to the demands of the husband's occupation was a prominent theme in the Pahls' study of middle managers and their wives (1971, pp. 258-9):

> ...willing slaves to the system...they suffer the full force of the competitive society they support. The sales manager must work on his books over the weekend because his opposite number in a rival firm is doing the same.

Willing or not, employing organisations tend not to rely upon the employee's perception of economic sanctions. They are fully alive to the need to inculcate as far as possible complete identification with the organisation, whatever the rank of the employee (Mills, 1956; Whyte, 1961). In a study of mid-career managers, Sofer found that organisations make considerable efforts in this direction, with the result that the majority of employees eventually feel thoroughly bound up with the organisation (1970, p. 340).

> Individuals who enter and remain in work organisations accordingly occupy roles which have embedded in them a contribution to some centrally defined objectives. Either they must accept those objectives as their own or go through the motions consistent with the attainment of those objectives, a process which tends in itself to turn into the commitment which they may have originally intended only to simulate.

Since the individuals to whom Sofer is referring are all husbands, it follows that their subordination to work organisations implies in every case the subordination of wives to the same organisations. Although Sofer reports that a large minority of wives objected to the demanding nature of their husband's work, he does not develop the discussion of this issue at all (ibid., pp. 195-7).

Robertson's (1975) study of young married couples in which the fathers were either hospital doctors or general dental practitioners found that there was a tendency for the former to be characterised by a 'work-centred' marital partnership and the latter by a more 'family-centred' marital partnership. The organisation of family life around the exigencies of the hospital doctor's work career, plus his very heavy workload, seemed to restrict home leisure and conjugal communication and had a marked effect on the wife's role, giving it a subordinate and supportive character. In another study of middle-class couples, Cohen (1977) found that the career pressures on husbands caused them to be absent from the home frequently. For couples at the child-rearing stage of the family cycle who lived on a housing estate, this pattern of absentee husbands had distinct consequences for the mother's socialisation role and life-style.

An alternative source of supporting data is studies of migration, widely regarded as a key feature of modern society that is especially pertinent to a study that includes salaried professional workers. In general, studies of migration indicate that the overwhelming reason for moving in the case of all occupational groups involves occupational achievement in some sense (Jackson, 1969; Jansen, 1970; Castles and Kosack, 1973). As far as professional workers are concerned, research shows that they are typically prepared to move more frequently and greater distances than most other occupational groups (Rose, 1958; Jansen, 1968). In the case of Bott's small-scale study, it was found that 'many of the professional couples had moved frequently from one local area to another and even from one city to another, and they tended to treat the requirements of the husband's career as the most important factor in deciding whether to move or not' (1971, p. 108).

The value of Turner's analysis can also be judged by comparing it to the recent work of Young and Willmott (1973). Young and Willmott surveyed the work, family and leisure relationships of a large number of couples in the London region. Like Turner and many others (Dubin, 1956; Orzack, 1959), they note the centrality of work in industrial societies. Unlike Turner, they fail to develop the point in any constructive or substantial way (1973, p. 151):

Whether or not labour is, in Marx's term, 'a commodity', it is a link with the collective life. Work also creates an ordering of the sort that is necessary not only to social structure. Routines in the way people organise their lives are indispensable to almost everyone. Work may not be essential for that. To provide a counterpoint between effort and relaxation, people invent such structures for themselves, for instance in retirement, when these are not forced upon them. But for most people an element of imposition, of external compulsion over the regularity of their daily lives, seems to make any freedom they have within it more attractive, or (to be negative about it) more bearable.

Young and Willmott amass considerable evidence to demonstrate that : the demands of work, especially on husbands, dominate family life. They do not systematically relate this material to the patterning of conjugal relationships, except to repeat their doubtful thesis that such relationships are becoming more symmetrical.[4] For example, much of their data on the long working hours of the 'higher classes' and the shiftwork of the manual workers strongly suggest that most husbands in their study were 'sacrificing their families to get money to support them' (ibid., p. 175).

In sharp contrast, Turner considers the consequences of what Young and Willmott tend to take for granted, namely, the subordination of family life to economic life (1970, p. 263).

> The authority of the husband to direct certain family decisions is therefore much more than simply adherence to a traditional belief in male authority but a product of the institutionalised subordination of the family to economic life. And the latter subordination is more than merely a matter of tradition; it rests on the fact that the irreducible base of family life as we know it is economic. Without the removal of this economic base ... it is difficult to see how a breadwinner can fail to carry authority in the family.

In other words, in a society in which the husband-father is established as the main economic role player, and the wife-mother as the main domestic role-player, a basic sexual division of labour is ensured. This largely ascriptive structure of relationships has significant implications for the patterning of conjugal roles. More specifically, a hierarchy of dependence is created in which husbands, by virtue of their 'instrumental' role, are directly dependent upon capital. The wives, in turn, are directly dependent upon their husbands. Thus under the present institutional arrangements, the subordination of family life to economic life becomes in practice the subordination of married women to their husbands. From time to time, even Young and Willmott concede that wives seek their husband's approval to go out to work and that often wives are 'controlled' by their husbands (1973, pp. 100-2).

In the light of what some may regard as the boldness of some of these assertions and in advance of a more detailed analysis, it is perhaps appropriate to introduce briefly some data to illustrate a few of the ways that professional workers and their wives conform to this hierarchy of dependence.

With every research couple, the whole topic of moving, changing jobs, overtime and the husband's periodic absence from the home were discussed at some length. Interestingly, the residential location of all the research families after marriage was determined by the husband's work career. In fact in the case of the professional workers in industry, most of them had moved frequently in response to direct requests from their employers, notwithstanding objections from their wives on many occasions. In addition to this general tendency to disrupt family and community relationships (largely in response to the husband's definition of the needs of his career), the data below indicate the range and extent of the subordination of family life to economic life.

She did not mind until the last move. She was worried about the children's education, I wanted to go higher up the ladder. She said: 'If you like the job I'll manage the children and the children will manage.' She has always given me one hundred per cent support in every way... Most difficult time in whole marriage, difficult job here seven days a week, fourteen hours a day, on continuous call all day and night. Her attitude was that one place is as good as another.   (Industrial Scientist)

The first thing I would want in moving is an interesting job allied to money... I think my wife thinks I spend too much time on work. She occasionally objects to me working in the evenings but not very often. She also objects to me going in at weekends and particularly in the last few years since I've been spending a lot of my time at meetings travelling around the world. I don't object particularly, I enjoy about two-thirds of them. I enjoy the break, travelling, but most of all meeting new faces and seeing how the world is running. This year about one day each week and one whole week each year and this year about one month away on courses. It causes difficulties at home because my wife has to go out teaching and I'm the babysitter and I'm not there. She had to organise it which isn't always easy and there is nobody to look after the children's homework.   (Industrial Scientist)

He goes away a lot. Once a week or about two days a week for half the year to me seems a lot. I used to mind when he started it, I was frightened at being alone at night. You get used to it and each time we have moved I've lived alone with the children for about six months.   (Industrial Scientist's Wife)

I don't mind now, used to when the children were small. Now I feel it is a nuisance. He doesn't get enough rest... Don't mind if he brings work home, used to it, but when we were first married I felt neglected, peeved. Realise it was necessary. He returns home about six to six-thirty most evenings.   (Industrial Scientist's Wife)

I don't regret it, but I always miss him very much when he is away, and sometimes think 'You lucky old so and so', if he is staying somewhere nice. It is part of his job, this is it so I don't regret it. As the children get older it does get easier because I'm not tied to the house . . . [Work at home] I accept this as part of our life, particularly if he is writing papers and is very busy I would do all I can to lighten his burden.   (Industrial Scientist's Wife)

He is always so involved in what he is doing. Not much time for anything else . . . He goes away and that's all right . . . But if I want to get away and I have to look after the children, I get a bit fed up.   (Academic's Wife)

I have achieved what I set out to achieve. If when I was older I wanted to pack up my practice I would expect my wife to fit into what I felt was in our best interest.   (Dentist)

She is not very interested in my work at all. I feel she could achieve more though if she tried to help me in my work instead of trying to get me away from my work . . . [Work at home] Most evenings if I'm not going out, I enjoy going through [house and surgery are part of the same building] . . . After all, it is my little kingdom. This is where I make my living and it's my little world.   (Dentist)

Among other things, these extracts show that the domination of family life by economic life can take various forms. Everything from the timing of the evening meal to where a couple live is susceptible to the husband's occupational career activities. In certain respects, the husband has only minimal choice in his *modus operandi* once he has entered a specific occupational culture. The data also suggest that this order of priorities is accorded legitimacy by both husbands and wives. Dissatisfaction regarding any inconvenience caused by the demands of the husband's work tends to be rationalised as inevitable. Some wives even express guilt about minding too much, while others feel quite proud that they can cope with the situation. In general, though, the main tendency is for both husbands and wives to acquiesce over time. In the process they come to define the situation as one in which they have to do all the adjusting rather than vice versa.

The different ways and extent to which wives are affected by and relate to their husband's work careers is demonstrated by Blood and Wolfe (1960). First, throughout their study the husband's occupation is repeatedly shown to be a crucial variable in the understanding of various aspects of marriage, including household task participation, decision-making and the wife's employment status. Secondly, their analysis of informative, friendship and colleague companionship shows that the majority of wives like to be told about their husband's work and share their husband's work colleagues and other friends. However, this particular aspect of Blood and Wolfe's work is seriously flawed by a highly sexist approach to the issue of marital companionship, both in the sense of being male-oriented and in the sense of assuming that things to do with the world of the male are more important than things to do with the world of the female. For example, three of Blood and Wolfe's four types of companionship were defined exclusively in terms of the wife's relationship to her husband's 'world'. Thus, how much a husband told his wife about his work was used to measure informative companionship; frequency of visiting the husband's workmates was used to judge colleague companionship; and the number of the husband's male friends known to the wife was used to assess friendship companionship (Blood and Wolfe, 1960, pp. 152-3).

In the present study of professional workers and their wives, data were also available on general attitudes towards sexual equality and some of these are presented below.

It would destroy femininity.   (Industrial Scientist's Wife)

In marriage men and women inherently have different functions to fulfil.   (Industrial Scientist)

Each sex has its own specific function, they should not try to perform each other's.   (Industrial Scientist's Wife)

Women generally like to be managed by men, this is instinctive.   (Industrial Scientist)

With equality, courtesies and manners towards women would disappear and I enjoy being a woman.   (Industrial Scientist's Wife)

I would not like my boss to be a woman.   (Academic)

Most women would become too hard and lose sight of the fact that they were female.   (Dentist's Wife)

There are basic physical and mental differences whether we like it or not. I want my woman to be female, not unisex.   (Dentist)

These and other similar responses revealed that approximately half the husbands and nearly two-thirds of the wives regarded sexual equality as a 'bad thing'. It is perhaps salutary to consider that these comments were elicited from couples who are often referred to as the 'emancipated' middle classes (Goode, 1970, p. 373). Moreover, elsewhere there was little evidence of a challenge to sex role norms. During the interviews I asked the couples about their hopes and aspirations for their children. The question was phrased in very general terms and provoked a rash of sexually differentiated expectations.

A happy family life and a rewarding career, but I have daughters so probably a happy family life.   (Father)

The girls, marriage or work. The boy, a career more.   (Mother)

A career is more important for sons than daughters, marriage is more important for girls.   (Father)

I would like the daughter [*sic*] to be happily married and have children and for John to do what he wants to do.   (Wife)

I think one has always got higher expectations for a son, a father must have, I think.   (Father)

Essential for boys to have a good education, less important for girls.   (Mother)

I would like one to be a doctor very much and for Susan to grow up into a lady. Nothing else. Also I would like grandchildren. (Mother)

The boy I would like to have some sort of qualification because it is going to be his livelihood. The girl I would like to have something because it is nice to have something to fall back on.   (Wife)

These attitudes may be pragmatically congruent with the tendency for husbands to be mainly responsible for financial support and for wives to be mainly responsible for the home, but at the same time they represent an essentially rigid and 'traditional' view of sex roles that is not very encouraging for the possibility of change in the future.

In conclusion, the above analysis suggests that the basic sex role structure which allocates a breadwinner role to husbands and a homemaking role to wives is increasingly difficult to justify, yet is widely accepted and involves the subordination of the home, and therefore women, to work, and therefore men. This prevailing division of labour is the context in which conjugal roles are organised. The exact implications of this highly differentiated sexual division of labour for the patterning of conjugal roles among professional workers and their wives at the child-rearing stage of the family cycle remain to be elucidated along with the possible influence of other factors.

Notes: Chapter 3

1 According to Parsons (1964, p. 422), there is another 'basic limitation' on absolute equality of opportunity and that is the tendency for all the members of the same conjugal family to share the same community status and its advantages/disadvantages, deserved or otherwise.

2 The rest of this study is largely concerned with this and related issues.

3 Two exceptions to this point are Harris (1969) and Robertson (1975).

4 Young and Willmott define symmetry as 'no monopolies for either sex in any sphere' (1973, p. 275). For a fuller discussion of Young and Willmott's symmetrical family thesis, see Chapter 5.

CHAPTER 4

The Household Division of Labour

The household division of labour refers to domestic and child-care tasks. This chapter is concerned with the extent of conjugal role segregation in these two areas of behaviour and an investigation into the factors that influence the household division of labour among professional workers and their wives at the child-rearing stage of the family cycle. With the aid of questionnaires administered to husbands and wives, data were collected on both domestic and child-care behaviour.[1] Tasks that were never shared were classed as segregated and tasks that were shared equally were classed as joint. Tasks that were 'mostly' undertaken by one of the spouses were classed as segregated to an intermediate degree. As in the case of Bott (1971) and many other researchers, I used three degrees of conjugal role segregation and, following the convention adopted by Turner (1967) among others, if the majority of responses were segregated, or intermediate, or joint, then the couple were regarded as having a predominantly segregated, or intermediate, or joint pattern of domestic task or child-care behaviour. In the few instances in which no one pattern predominated, qualitative data were used to resolve the issue.[2] Husband and wife scores were combined because discrepancies were few in number, small in scale and tended overall to cancel each other out. The organisation of the data in this way showed that every research family was characterised by a predominantly segregated or intermediate pattern of domestic task behaviour, and that a majority of couples were characterised by a predominantly segregated or intermediate pattern of child-care behaviour. The exact breakdown of the figures is shown in Table 4.1. The table indicates a marked lack of conjugal role jointness in domestic task behaviour and shows that only a minority of couples are characterised by conjugal role jointness in child-care behaviour. These findings confirm what others have found, namely, that husbands tend to participate more in child-care tasks than in domestic tasks and that high levels of husband participation in the latter are conspicuously absent (Oakley, 1974). This overwhelming evidence of conjugal role segregation, especially in domestic task behaviour, could be said to reflect the profound influence of the sexual division of labour in which men are typically responsible for the

Table 4.1   *Degree of Conjugal Role Segregation and the Household Division of Labour*

| | Degree of Conjugal Role Segregation | | |
| | Segregated | Intermediate | Joint |
	No. (%)	No. (%)	No. (%)
Domestic tasks	18 (47)	20 (53)	0 (0)
Child-care tasks	6 (16)	15 (39)	17 (45)

breadwinning role and women for homemaking. Moreover this pattern of conjugal role segregation is entirely congruent with the sex role norms expressed by most of the research couples. Parallel findings are also reported by Robertson (1975) in her study of doctors and dentists and their wives. She found that husband participation in domestic and child-care tasks was extremely low in terms of hours and suggests that this is to be expected in households in which husbands, in contrast to wives, are absent for most of the day.

The next step was to discover whether or not segregation in one part of the household division of labour was accompanied by segregation in the other. Further analysis of the basic data on the incidence of domestic task and child-care behaviour among the research couples revealed that there was no association between the degree of conjugal role segregation in the two areas of family life (Table 4.2). This directly supports Oakley's view that it is not possible to predict a couple's degree of conjugal role segregation in one area from their degree of conjugal role segregation in another (1974, p. 139).

Table 4.2   *The Degree of Conjugal Role Segregation in Domestic Tasks and Child-Care Tasks*

| | Degree of Conjugal Role Segregation in Domestic Tasks | | |
Degree of conjugal role segregation in child-care	Segregated No. (%)	Intermediate No. (%)	Joint No. (%)
Segregated	3 (8)	3 (8)	0 (0)
Intermediate	5 (13)	10 (26.3)	0 (0)
Joint	10 (26.3)	7 (18.3)	0 (0)

Apart from the fundamental and pervasive influence of the prevailing sexual division of labour that consigns wives to the home and high levels of domestic labour and husbands to work outside the home and low levels of domestic labour, it remains to be seen what other factors are associated with what Bott has called 'variation of detail' (1971, p. 54) in the degree of conjugal role segregation. Three of the most frequently mentioned factors are geographical and occupational mobility and social network connectedness (Bott, 1971; Turner, 1967; Harris, 1970).

In the research study, a map of every family's social network was produced on the basis of the interview data provided by the spouses. It was found that, irrespective of the extent of geographical mobility of the focal couple, every research family was characterised by a predominantly loose-knit social network.[3] The main reasons for this concerned the migratory style of the 'middle-class' life-cycle which entails moving house for whatever reasons and travelling, often quite great distances, to work, visit friends and relatives, engage in various social activities, and so on. The effect of all this movement was to generate a highly dispersed and fluid social network. Thus, despite the residential stability of any one focal couple, the combined and cumulative forces of geographical mobility among their friends and relatives, and the specialisation characteristic of their work and non-work activities invariably led to the development of a decidedly loose-knit social network among the burgesses as well as the spiralists—a possibility that was fully appreciated by Bott. 'Even if the family itself does not move, its network will become less connected if friends and relatives move away' (1971, p. 108). The only apparent difference was that some couples tended to develop one or two local segments that were relatively close-knit, such as a coterie of neighbourhood friends or professional colleagues. However, this was usually in the context of decreasing connectedness over time for the professional workers and their wives in this sample.

A major implication of this finding is that the distinction between burgess and spiralist would not seem to be crucial to social network density. It seemed to take only a small amount of geographical mobility among a few families for a professional couple's total network to become loose-knit. In the light of the finding that every research family was characterised by a predominantly loose-knit social network it was not possible to examine variations in social network connectedness in relation to the patterning of conjugal role behaviour. Furthermore, the findings of this study throw considerable doubt on the validity of Bott's famous hypothesis linking the degree of conjugal role segregation with social network density.

An investigation of the research study material on inter- and intragenerational occupational mobility[4] and geographical mobility also produced largely negative though none the less instructive results. First, no systematic relationship was found between the patterning of domestic tasks or child-care behaviour and the incidence of geographical mobility experienced by each couple. This is perhaps not too surprising in view of the already noted predominantly loose-knit character of every couple's social network, but it does reinforce the conclusion regarding the irrelevance of the burgess/spiralist distinction to the study of conjugal role segregation among professional workers and their wives.[5] Secondly, in the case of occupational mobility, there was evidence of a slight association between the patterning of conjugal role behaviour and the experience of mobility, but only with reference to child-care tasks. For example, the greater the career mobility of the husband, the more segregated the child-care behaviour, especially among the most upwardly mobile husbands intragenerationally. However, the high number of negative cases compared to the small size of the total non-random sample considerably reduced the import of this finding. In the main, therefore, it is difficult to avoid the conclusion that, as conventionally measured, types of occupational mobility alone seem not to be clearly related to the degree of segregation in the household division of labour among professional workers and their wives at the child-rearing stage of the family cycle. At the same time, there is the suggestion that it would be somewhat premature to reject outright the earlier hypothesis that a husband's orientation to his occupational career influences the patterning of conjugal role behaviour.

In order to explore further this and other possibilities both occupational and family career stages were investigated. Historically, the term 'career' refers to bureaucratic employment in which an individual moves from lower to higher positions (Weber, 1961); but recently it has been widely used to denote any 'series of related and definable stages or phases of a given activity that a person goes through on his way to a more or less definite and recognisable end point or goal' (Roth, 1963, p. 144). In this more recent sense, the term career has been applied to an increasingly wide variety of contexts including family life in addition to professional work (Sofer, 1970; Elliott, 1972; Rodgers, 1964; Rowe, 1966).[6] These and other studies not only demonstrate the usefulness of the notion family career but also provide evidence for the view that family careers are relevant to an understanding of conjugal roles. More specifically, there is the suggestion that the combination of a husband's involvement in a professional work career and the wife's preoccupation with a domestic role, especially during the early pre-school phase, favour a segregated conjugal role structure (Edgell, 1970).

Three work career stages were distinguished according to the husband's age and three family career stages according to the age of the first child. These work and family career stages are similar to those used in other studies, but modified to take into account the specific character and focus of this study (Gerstl and Hutton, 1966; Rowe, 1966). For example, restricting the sample to children living at home produced a shortage of families in the late work career category and consequently necessitated limiting the mid-career stage to husbands aged between 35 and 40 years old. By the same token child-rearing is often treated as a single stage in other studies but in this project it is divided into three phases. Thus, early, mid- and late work career stages (Table 4.3) and young, mid- and late family career stages (Table 4.4) were delineated and examined in relation to the household division of labour.

Table 4.3   *Work Career Stages and the Household Division of Labour*

Husband's work career stage	Domestic task pattern			Child-care task pattern		
	Segregated	Intermed.	Joint	Segregated	Intermed.	Joint
Early	6	7	0	2	8	3
Middle	5	5	0	2	0	8
Late	7	8	0	2	7	6

Table 4.4   *Family Career Stages and the Household Division of Labour*

Family career stage	Domestic task pattern			Child-care task pattern		
	Segregated	Intermed.	Joint	Segregated	Intermed.	Joint
Young	5	7	0	2	7	3
Middle	8	7	0	2	4	9
Late	5	6	0	2	4	5

The data on work and family career stages and the household division of labour indicate no distinct pattern in the case of domestic task behaviour. It is segregated to a greater or lesser extent throughout both the work and family career-cycles. However, in the case of child-care behaviour the data shows that conjugal role jointness in this area is more common during mid-career than at any other work and family career stage. This tendency for child-care jointness to increase after the first work and family career stages and decline slightly during the late career stages suggests that the impact of primary sex role obligations is relevant but uneven. Thus, when the data were examined further, it was found that during the early work and family career stages most husbands were highly involved in their professional careers and that correspondingly the wives were highly involved in their household activities, especially child-care tasks. The three early career exceptions could be said to be quite atypical and therefore do not contradict the overall impression that a spouse's involvement in work and family roles influences the patterning of conjugal behaviour in certain respects. For example, in one of the early career negative cases, the wife worked full-time outside the home due to financial pressures (research family no. 19). In a second case the husband had already experienced considerable occupational career mobility and during the husband-only interview conceded that although he was still ambitious, his opportunities for promotion were slim (research family no. 24). Finally, the other early career exception concerned a self-employed dentist who had followed his father into the profession and the business (research family no. 34). This respondent was unusual in that his level of work career commitment was relatively low and his family situation seemed to be characterised by a marked lack of economic necessity.

During mid-career the tendency was for an increasing number of husbands to experience a rise in their participation in child-care tasks. This seemed to be associated with a decline in the husband's work career involvement and a greater compatibility between the father and child diurnal 'work' schedules and leisure interests. However, if the factors more commonly experienced during the early work and family career stages persist, such as the husband's high degree of commitment to his professional work career and/or the presence of additional pre-school children, then a more segregated household division of labour seems likely to prevail.

This pattern of work and family career-structured influences was found to extend into the third and final parental stage. This stage is typically one in which husbands tend to reduce, and wives tend to increase, their respective levels of occupational career involvement. For example, among the couples who were characterised by a predominantly joint pattern of child-care behaviour during this late work and family career stage were a husband who was near retirement (research family no. 4), a husband who had become decisively blocked in his professional career and whose wife was not fully fit (research family no. 6) and a wife who worked full-time outside the home (research family no. 21). Once again, however, there were several exceptions and these mainly reflected the continued persistence of factors more usually associated with previous work and family career stages.

Overall these findings suggest that family variables are as relevant as (male) work variables to an understanding of conjugal role behaviour. Consequently the tentative hypothesis noted earlier concerning a husband's orientation to success at work and the patterning of conjugal role relationships is supported by the data from this study but only partially. This factor is certainly important, but it operates in conjunction with other factors. In other words, it needs to be supplemented by, at the very least, reference to family variables and in particular the stage in the family life-cycle. The latter seems to affect both spouses' child-care behaviour in the context of an otherwise highly differentiated sexual division of labour.

This work and family career stage model contains a number of negative cases. Further analysis suggested that the leisure interests of each spouse were also relevant to the patterning of conjugal roles. In fact the idea that an individual's interest in one sphere of activity, say, work, family life or leisure, can influence his or her behaviour in other spheres is widely recognised in sociology (for example: Dubin, 1956; Orzack, 1959; Salvo, 1969; Parker, 1972). In this research tradition, work or occupation is a standard independent variable by virtue of its economic, political and social importance in the lives of individuals and groups. However, in many of the occupational typologies that are used, there is a tendency to lump together and regard as more satisfying those occupations that involve greater pecuniary rewards, prestige, and the manipulation of people and symbols; and to regard as less satisfying those occupations that involve relatively small incomes, low status and the manipulation of physical objects. In general the assumption is that manual work is less intrinsically meaningful than non-manual work. For example, in Parker's theory of work and leisure, professional workers are clearly assumed to be highly involved in their occupations in a positive way, whereas manual workers are thought to be engaged in uninteresting and unpleasant work. As a direct consequence of these assumed work experiences, professional workers are thought to have 'extension' leisure pursuits and manual workers are thought to have 'opposition' leisure patterns (Parker, 1972). Whatever the empirical validity of these broad work and leisure relationships, the theory tends to systematically undervalue the possibility that some forms of manual work are physically and socially satisfying (for instance, bricklaying), and overvalue the intrinsic and extrinsic rewards of non-manual work.[7]

In the same way that one cannot assume that all professional workers, male or female, are equally interested and involved in their work careers, one cannot assume that all married women experience in the same way their family careers. Similarly, there is evidence from this and other studies to suggest that leisure is a salient area of life that varies from one individual to another in terms of its centrality and impact on other areas of family life, including conjugal role behaviour. In order to be able to explore these lines of thought, all the research couples characterised by a predominantly joint pattern of child-care behaviour were separated out from the rest of the sample. The two groups of families were examined with reference to the work, family and leisure interests of each spouse. A thorough analysis of the interview data revealed that among the couples characterised by a predominantly joint pattern of child-care behaviour there was a marked tendency for the husbands to be less interested and involved in their work careers than the husbands in the group of families characterised by a predominantly segregated pattern of child-care behaviour. Secondly, the 'joint' child-care husbands tended to be more interested in leisure interests than the 'segregated' husbands. Thirdly, although all the wives indicated considerable interest in family life, those who were characterised by a joint pattern of child-care behaviour tended to have more non-family interests and activities, such as work outside the home and/or leisure, than those characterised by a predominantly segregated pattern of child-care behaviour. Illustrative case-study data are presented below in support of these broad yet complex relationships between the work, family and leisure interests and involvements of professional workers and their wives, and the household division of labour.

Couples with a predominantly segregated household division of labour

Research family no. 28 is fairly typical of the couples in this category. Mr Newton is a highly committed university lecturer and his wife is a full-time mother and housewife with few interests and activities outside the home.

Mr Newton:
Family life is often geared to work. I come home late, and I'm not there for meals twice a week at least. Often have to phone up and say I'll be late, and at weekends sometimes I have extra work to get done . . . There is always something new and stimulating at work. I couldn't stand being at home all day. I've always studied at home; wife was conditioned to it from the start. I just like my work, better than a job isn't it? . . . The area we live in is important . . . [probe] Job is more important really, in deciding where to move to.

Mrs Newton: (husband's work involvement, including work at home and courses/conferences away from home)
Oh it's good. It is good for him. It's refreshing and I don't mind being alone. It's part of his job and I accept it. He enjoys his work and that is the most important thing . . . I don't particularly want a career. At this particular stage in our lives we have decided to have children and I can best help our marriage by being at home and doing the work around the home . . . I like to do a fair amount of cooking . . . I make most of my own clothes and most of Jane's [daughter]; so that takes time. I don't make a fetish of cleaning— get it done. Doesn't bother me, someone has to do it and it's got to be done.

The Newtons had recently moved to the north of England and they were both preoccupied with their respective roles outside and inside the home. Consequently, neither of them seemed to have the inclination or the time to develop interests beyond their roles as primary breadwinner and primary homemaker. Mrs Newton 'always' did all the cooking, cleaning and laundry and most of the washing-up, shopping and child-related household tasks. Mr Newton was mainly but not solely responsible for the maintenance of the house and the household budget. The care of the garden and playing with the children were essentially joint activities. Mr Newton claimed not to be very ambitious but was none the less highly involved in all aspects of his professional work career. He spoke long and enthusiastically about his research, his teaching and the fact that he did more than his fair share of administration in his academic department. Neither of the Newtons experienced his or her major role responsibilities as boring. Mrs Newton noted: 'I haven't had a chance yet. I've always so many things to do.' Mr Newton responded in a similar way when we discussed the possibility of more leisure time and longer holidays: 'I don't distinguish between work and non-work really, so I can hardly conceive that it would make any difference.' At this point during the joint interview Mrs Newton interjected: 'I would like more free time together, but his work is so important and it is part of our lives.' In this family Mrs Newton collaborated in her husband's subordination to his work career, and therefore the family's subordination to the same exigency. In the relative absence of alternative interests, work dominated the husband's life and domestic work dominated the wife's.

In many families the extent of conjugal role segregation was often revealed by the manner in which work roles were described and the amount of time, energy and other resources husbands and wives devoted to them. For example, husbands would refer to 'my work', meaning their work career, and 'the children'. Wives tended to refer to 'my work', meaning housework, and 'my children'. Mrs Edwards was the wife of an industrial scientist (research family no. 14), and described her role in this way. Mrs Edwards was 37 years old and had not worked since marriage. She said that she had 'no desire at all' to go out to work again, adding that she was 'too happy at home. I like all the things connected with being at home—apart from cleaning.' Mrs Edwards regarded domestic work as 'interesting, worthwhile, enjoyable and satisfying' and virtually all her social activities were oriented to her home role, including cooking, sewing and knitting. Finally, the only magazines and journals that I noticed lying around the house were mass circulation weeklies for women, of which there were many.

Another couple with a predominantly segregated pattern of child-care and domestic task conjugal behaviour were research family no. 1. Mrs Conner described her daily routine in some detail and with not a little enthusiasm, and summed up by noting: 'I like to have the house spotless all the time and I'm never bored at home.' Mrs Conner stated that she 'reads lots of recipes', cooks 'two new meals a week', tries to 'vary the diet' and bakes 'a lot'. For his part, Mr Conner was very ambitious and claimed that if he won the pools, he would 'continue working' because 'work is interesting and I would regress, no aims in life, become a cabbage'. In terms of their respective 'wishes', Mr Conner was unusual in that he did not mention his family at all. Instead he stated that he wanted 'to be successful in my job', 'win a large sum of money' and 'speak a foreign language'. In contrast, and less unusually, all Mrs Conner's 'wishes' involved her family.

Comments by highly involved professional workers (husbands) ranged from claims like 'Work is my life' (research family no. 35) to statements like 'I wouldn't want a job that wasn't demanding intellectually' (research family no. 9). When deciding upon a new job, such husbands typically expressed the view that they put their work careers before all else. As Mr Dyer (research family no. 13), and many other husbands, said: 'My career comes first.'

A good example of a husband for whom work was highly salient and whose household division of labour was distinctively segregated was Mr Vernon (research family no. 37). Mr Vernon was a self-employed dentist who described how much he enjoyed his work and how he found it difficult to distinguish between work and non-work. His surgery was on the same premises as his home and he said that he 'drifted back most evenings'.

Generally husbands and wives for whom 'work' was a major interest tended to have fewer non-work and non-domestic-work interests compared to those couples for whom 'work' was not their sole major interest. For example, Mr Parker (research family no. 30) worked very long hours on his thesis and lecture notes and consequently, apart from family holidays, he seemed to have very little leisure time and participated in only a small way in the home. A good indication of one husband's level of work involvement was his frequent absence from the home on business, often at short notice, that meant he was reluctant to develop any regular non-work commitments. In one case (research family no. 20) several appointments to interview the husband had to be cancelled before a mutually convenient time was achieved. The wives in this group of 'segregated' couples also tended to have fewer non-work interests, that is, interests outside their domestic work and child-care activities. For example, Mrs Roberts (research family no. 33), although an extreme case, conformed to the pattern very clearly. Mrs Roberts seemed so involved in her homemaking role that even the advantage of being able to afford domestic help had not led to an increase in non-domestic-work interests and activities. When leisure interests were discussed it transpired that Mrs Roberts rarely went out except to walk her dog, had only one friend whom she occasionally accompanied to the cinema or theatre, and had no other leisure interests apart from the television and playing games such as table tennis and cards with her children.

Significantly, work was not a major interest for all the husbands, whereas domestic work was a major interest for all the wives who were interviewed. Husbands tended to have more interests outside their professional work careers. This suggests that the domestic role for married women is far more difficult to 'escape' from than the work role is for married men. This may have something to do with the spatial separation of home from work for most men and the lack of spatial separation of home from domestic work for women and the ascription of child-care responsibility to the wives. It could also stem from socialisation and the social unacceptability of women in public places. Furthermore, it could be interpreted to mean that married men have the 'power' to choose between competing spheres of action, but that married women either do not have the same degree of 'power' or that they elect not to use it. A fuller analysis of this particular point is undertaken in subsequent chapters. Here it is relevant to note that marriage and family roles were generally of greater significance to married women than to married men in this sample. This confirms the findings of other studies that interestingly have arrived at a broadly similar conclusion though usually via a different route (Fogarty, Rapoport and Rapoport, 1971; Pahl and Pahl, 1971; Hart, 1973).

Couples with a predominantly joint pattern of child-care behaviour

In contrast to the families discussed above, the couples with a predominantly joint pattern of child-care behaviour tended to show a greater interest in non-work and non-domestic-work activities. Also in the case of the husbands, the vast majority were less involved in their professional work careers than the husbands with a predominantly segregated pattern of child-care behaviour. This increase in husband participation in child-care activities, and in some cases domestic tasks as well, seemed to be due to a relative decline in the interest shown by husbands and wives in their otherwise quite salient breadwinning and homemaking roles.

Sometimes this more shared child-care pattern was occasioned by the husband's increasing dissatisfaction with his work career. For example, Mr Bond (research family no. 10) expressed this view and explained that this was 'because I am not collecting information any more'. When pressed, Mr Bond stated: 'Previously I was always gaining information, now I'm just pouring it out, gradually being emptied. Work is less interesting. I'm acting as a bank, pouring out money and not gaining very much.' Apart from the inaccuracy of the metaphor, Mr Bond closely resembled the once intrinsically involved industrial scientist who had become dissatisfied by middle age (Cotgrove and Box, 1970, p. 132). As a consequence of this changed attitude towards work, Mr Bond was less inclined to 'bring work home', 'go in at weekends', and was certainly not eager to move again. On the other hand, he said that he and his wife had 'talked about the children a lot and have decided that we both have equal responsibility for playing and bringing up children'. However, although Mr Bond had increased his level of participation in child-care activities, domestic task behaviour remained markedly segregated and unequal, despite Mrs Bond's recent return to work outside the home.

Another case that illustrates some of the possible ways in which changes in the salience of different social spheres can influence the organisation of selected aspects of conjugal behaviour concerns research family no. 38. Mr Wade was a dentist in general practice. Mrs Wade was a mother and housewife who was also an extremely busy local politician. During the course of his work career, Mr Wade had become increasingly disenchanted with dentistry and correspondingly more and more involved in his leisure and family life. In many important respects Mr Wade had a markedly instrumental orientation to work, an orientation that is more usually associated with manual work (Goldthorpe *et al.*, 1968, pp. 38-9).[8]

I have often thought about another career, such as teaching or
flying aeroplanes . . . went back to studying about six months ago.
Thought it would give me some indication as to whether I would
enjoy going back to bookwork again. As it happened, there were so
many commitments, family and work, that I gave up the evening
class. But the general impression I got was that I would not enjoy an
academic career . . . I always look at the adverts to see what jobs are
going . . . This year I have worked four days a week. At the moment
I'm trying to prune my workload so that I can take two weeks off
in August. I take all the half-terms the children have, but during
term times we can't take long weekends. At forty I am now resigned
to carry on with dentistry. I don't know what else I could do at this
late stage . . . I want satisfaction from dentistry but I also get bored.
Because of my personal commitments, money does loom very large
all the time. Money matters an awful lot because of the particular
circumstances.

In general Mr Wade was somewhat disenchanted with his work career:
'It hasn't lived up to its expectations. I found it very much harder than
I anticipated. Not the physical discomfort, the fatigue in general.' On
the other hand, Mr Wade's highly calculative attitude towards work
contrasted with his enthusiasm for leisure: 'I can't get enough holidays.' He also spoke about the need 'to get away to relax' at his
second home on the coast. Mr Wade was a keen golfer and swimmer
and attended keep fit classes, yet commented that he did not participate in these activities as frequently as he wished.

As far as domestic tasks were concerned, Mr Wade 'helped in the
house' only reluctantly: 'I can think of more interesting things than
washing dishes.' Mrs Wade had been ill in the past and was unable to
stand for long periods at a time. Although they employed a part-time
cleaner, Mr Wade expressed the view that he participated in domestic
tasks far more than he preferred. Mr Wade's level of domestic task
participation was in fact far from joint, yet he was clearly not satisfied about the extent of his domestic activity.

When you come home from work and there is no wife [due to ill-
health or council business], with two hungry kids you don't go off
and play golf or something. I would much prefer to, but it is a
question of necessity.

Mrs Wade did not want to have a work career, although she had
enjoyed working before marriage and still 'helps' her husband with his
'bookwork' (accounts). Mrs Wade's career before marriage was in
social work, specialising in child-care, and she expressed a professional interest in the context of her local political activities. In the case

of this particular family, the impression was that many of the changes in the organisation of the household division of labour were due to a combination of factors, notably Mr Wade's decline in work involvement and Mrs Wade's ill-health and voluntary work. The result had been an increase in the husband's participation in child-care and to a lesser extent in domestic tasks, much to his regret.

Among other joint child-care conjugal behaviour couples, the husbands often made reference to the demands of work organisations, especially those who were at or near the apex of the hierarchy. Typically it was mid-career husbands who seemed most aware of this problem. For example, in research family no. 8, Mr Ash, an industrial scientist, was concerned about the long hours 'top management' were expected to work:

> Once one gets to the very high levels, company expects more of your time. Become a company man. I'm not willing to be so much of a company man when I see our present top management staying until seven or eight in the evening and half the weekend. Not worth the sacrifice, quite honestly. It's the time factor. I feel I have a certain duty toward my family, and they expect to see a certain amount of me.

At this stage of his work career, Mr Ash said that he did less work at home although he still went on 'business trips' to Europe for his employers.

Mid-career is also a time when anxieties about the children's education seem to be most prominent. Often fear of disrupting their children's education was given as a reason for not wanting to move and/or experience promotion. In the case of Mr Jarvis (research family no. 21), an industrial scientist whose wife worked full-time as a teacher, the fact that his wife worked presented no problem, but the children did.

However, in many cases the husband regarded this situation as purely temporary. For example, in research family no. 8 quoted above, and in other research families, the husbands claimed that as soon as their children had completed their education they would be prepared once more to be mobile both geographically and occupationally. When this happens, the evidence suggests that, other things being equal, the degree of conjugal role-sharing in all areas of family life will tend to decline.

This finding is congruent with the fact that among the joint child-care couples, adherence to basic sex role norms was as widespread as it was among predominantly segregated child-care couples. In other words, although the husbands were less involved in their work careers and the wives had more interests and activities outside the home, couples characterised by a joint pattern of child-care behaviour none the less maintained that wives should be primarily responsible for the home and husbands should be mainly responsible for financial provision. For example, Mrs Moss (research family no. 6) described her role responsibilities solely in terms of domestic and child-care activities and ended the interview with the phrase 'my little home and family'. Similarly, Mr Ash (research family no. 8) was not alone when he expressed the view that work careers were more important for boys than girls, whilst Mrs Ash said that she would like one of her sons to be a doctor and for her daughter 'to grow into a lady'. Thus although the predominantly joint child-care couples had modified (some only temporarily) their otherwise highly differentiated sex roles, they continued to subscribe to the 'traditional' model in terms of both expectations and behaviour, especially in relation to domestic tasks.

Negative cases

Negative or deviant-case analysis (Denzin, 1970, p. 48) can sometimes lead to theoretical revision and it is for this reason that it is widely recognised as being an important part of the research process.[9]

The more detailed analysis of the salience of each spouse's work, family and leisure involvements has suggested that the more a couple develop interests outside their major breadwinner and homemaker role responsibilities, the less segregated the organisation of child-care tasks. The notable exception to this tendency was research family no. 27. Mr and Mrs Green both worked full-time outside the home and claimed that they could not manage their family roles without the extensive services of immediate kin (parents) who lived nearby. This suggests that the Greens' involvement in non-work activities could not be maintained in the absence of considerable financial, domestic and child-care kin aid. Kin aid among professional families would seem to be relevant not only to the recipients' standard of living, but to their style of living as well. Therefore, extensive kin aid has implications for work, family and leisure patterns, especially in facilitating the employment of married women, that are far less well documented than the exchange of financial help between generations (Bell, 1968a; Firth, Hubert and Forge, 1969).

There were other families who did not conform to the tendency for the organisation of the household division of labour to vary in relation to the spouses' interest in their respective 'work' roles compared to other social activities. In research family no. 3, the husband was a very ambitious industrial scientist (shortly after the completion of the field-work this family moved again) who was also active in local politics.

Mrs Jackson was a part-time teacher and was also active in a variety of local voluntary organisations. The Jacksons had four children in whom they took a great deal of interest. In research family no. 19 both the husband and wife worked full-time outside the home, although they both regarded Mr Harding as the major breadwinner in the long term. The Hardings had one pre-school child who attended a nursery full-time. In research family no. 32, the husband was an exceptionally committed professional worker who spent a considerable amount of his non-work time on his career, often away from home. Mrs Harvey was a full-time mother and housewife and, in addition to caring for her own five children, was a registered foster-mother.

Among the research families, these were undoubtedly three of the most energetic as indicated by their work, leisure and family activities. A careful examination of the data on these couples did not reveal any obvious differences between them and the other couples who were also characterised by a predominantly joint pattern of child-care conjugal behaviour. The general lack of any clues to the possible explanation of these negative cases could be interpreted in many ways. It could be that these couples were atypically efficient, or that the classification went awry. Either way, these cases could be interpreted as further evidence of the major significance of the basic sexual division of labour compared to the minor significance of the 'variations of detail' that this analysis has been mainly concerned to investigate. In practice all three couples conformed like all the other research couples to a highly differentiated sex role structure: the husband was regarded as the primary breadwinner and the wife the primary homemaker.

Summary and concluding remarks

The main finding of this chapter is that when professional workers and their wives are considered as individuals and examined from the standpoint of the comparative salience of their work, family and leisure activities, most of the variation in the organisation of their domestic task and child-care behaviour is accounted for. More specifically, the data suggest that the greater the interest spouses show in their primary roles of breadwinner and homemaker, compared to other social activities, the more segregated the couple's child-care behaviour. This confirms and extends the Rosser and Harris hypothesis that 'the more domesticated the women, the more involved they are in domestic affairs, the more "homely", the greater the likelihood of a sharp division of roles' (1965, p. 208). Rosser and Harris define domesticity as 'the degree of involvement and interest in domestic affairs and household skills' (ibid., p. 209); and in terms of the explanation of variations in conjugal role behaviour, the corollary of female domesticity is male involvement and interest in work outside the home.

An alternative way of summarising these findings is to suggest that the more a couple specialise and identify with 'traditional' sex roles, the more likely it is that their conjugal role behaviour, especially in child-care activities, will be predominantly segregated. Thus, the tentative hypothesis noted earlier regarding the effect of the husband's orientation to success at work on the organisation of conjugal roles (Edgell, 1970), would seem to be largely validated. However, it would also need, on the evidence of this study, to be qualified by a reference to the wife's orientation to 'domesticity', and to both spouses' interest and involvement in leisure activities.[10]

After examining the data from various points of view the inescapable conclusion is that Bott's central hypothesis concerning the tendency for 'the degree of segregation in the role-relationship of husband and wife' to vary 'directly with the connectedness of the family's social network' has to be rejected (1971, p. 60). Moreover, Bott's suggestion that 'professional or semi-professional people' are characterised by 'the most joint role-relationships' (although there were many exceptions in Bott's small-scale exploratory study), would also seem to be questionable in the light of the evidence of the present study (ibid., p. 56). Finally, the extent to which the majority of the research couples expressed support for traditional (i.e. highly differentiated) sex role norms is in line with the equally dominant tendency for the research couples to organise their household division of labour in an essentially segregated manner. In the case of domestic work, the tasks that husbands participated in most were those that may be regarded as traditionally masculine such as household repairs. Husbands also expressed a preference for certain child-care tasks, for instance, playing with children, rather than other tasks such as washing, ironing, mending and buying their clothes.

However, there are at least two important limitations to the material presented so far: first, the findings only relate to the household division of labour; and secondly, they only relate to professional workers and their wives at the child-rearing stage of the family life-cycle. The first point will be remedied in the next two chapters, the second will be discussed in the concluding chapter.

Notes: Chapter 4

1   House, garden and car maintenance were included along with the more usual range of domestic items such as cooking and cleaning. In all there were ten questions on domestic tasks (questions 2, 3, 4, 6, 7, 8, 9, 12, 26 and 27|on the questionnaire) and five on child-care tasks (questions 13, 14, 15, 16 and 22).

2 There were six cases in the category, all of which concerned child-care behaviour. Three were eventually classed as joint and three as intermediate on the basis of additional data such as the supervision of homework.

3 In some cases there was evidence of a small local core of social relationships which could be described as close-knit. For example, full-time housewives with pre-school children who lived on new housing estates often built up a small yet dense network of neighbourhood friends. In this connection see Cohen, 1977. However, such segments were invariably only a minor and often quite isolated part of any one couple's total social network.

4 No instances of downward occupational mobility were encountered among the selected research sample; consequently, all references to occupational mobility are implicitly references to upward mobility.

5 The Japanese data by Wimberley (1973) and the Scottish data by Robertson (1975) also support this conclusion which is of course contrary to the view expressed by Bott (1971, p. 267).

6 For example, the term 'career' has been used in the study of age-related careers (McCall and Simmons, 1966), moral careers (Goffman, 1968) and income careers (Lane, 1972).

7 I fully accept that in general manual work is more 'irksome' than non-manual work (Veblen, 1970) and typically far less well rewarded in a number of important respects. The point here is not to discount the possibility of, say, an industrial scientist experiencing work as an oppressive, routinised, exploitative activity, especially during the later stages of an occupational career.

8 Goldthorpe *et al.* (1968, pp. 38-9) define an instrumental orientation to work as one in which 'work is regarded as a means of acquiring the income necessary to support a valued way of life of which work itself is not an integral part'.

9 For example, Bott (1971, p. 312) has noted: 'Throughout any study I would keep a careful eye out for negative cases because they are likely to show one which variables are crucial and how they operate.'

10 This general line of reasoning is supported by Safilios-Rothschild (1970a), who found that a wife's degree of work commitment had more influence on certain aspects of family life than a wife's working status.

CHAPTER 5
Conjugal Power and Authority

At least four kinds of contribution are discernible in the large literature on marital power and authority in Western societies.[1] First, there are studies that focus on measurement problems and the construction of models (Foote, 1969; Safilios-Rothschild, 1969 and 1970b; Cromwell and Olson, 1975). Next there are studies that tend to argue from a historical perspective that 'modern marriage' is increasingly characterised by equality of power and authority (Blood and Wolfe, 1960; Fletcher, 1962; Burgess, Locke and Thomes, 1963; Parsons, 1964; Willmott, 1969; Young and Willmott, 1973). Thirdly, there are those who are highly critical of this view and instead maintain that marital relationships are still essentially unequal (Rossi, 1964; Goode, 1970; Turner, 1970; Gillespie, 1971; Bernard, 1973; Bell and Newby, 1976). Finally, there is the more overtly political literature, both Marxist and feminist, which is mainly concerned with the causes of sexual inequality and the steps needed to eradicate it (Engels, 1972; de Beauvoir, 1972; Rowbotham, 1973; Mitchell, 1974; Zaretsky, 1976).[2] The incorporation of radical ideas into the mainstream of academic sociology has only recently been undertaken, to the great advantage of sociology (Oakley, 1974; Middleton, 1974; Morgan, 1975; Hamilton, 1978).

Among other things, the more methodologically preoccupied contributions suggest that family power is a highly complex issue and that no one researcher can expect to examine all its many aspects (Cromwell and Olson, 1975). This being so, the methodological prescriptions of Safilios-Rothschild (1969 and 1970b) regarding the study of marital decision-making are particularly instructive. In a thorough review of family decision-making studies, Safilios-Rothschild contends that to improve the validity and comprehensiveness of research in this area data should be collected from both husbands and wives. Secondly, 'the entire range of common familial decisions' as reported and specified by respondents should be included, and 'each spouse's answers regarding the most influential decision-maker for each individual decision' and 'the importance accorded to the decision' should also be examined. Finally, Safilios-Rothschild suggests that 'the renewed frequency of the decision should be taken into account'.

The historically oriented studies tend to be inadequate in terms of this advice and many other criteria. Part of the problem is that the paucity of historical evidence does not seem to have discouraged certain writers from explicitly or implicitly contrasting the present with the past. For example, Burgess, Locke and Thomes (1963) emphasise that industrial urbanism is associated with the development of a more 'democratic' type of family in contrast to the 'authoritarian' structures of the 'past'. Similarly, Fletcher has written that in contemporary Britain the married couple 'are of equal status and expect to have an equal share in taking decisions' (1962, p. 130). This optimism is reminiscent of Parsons's essays (1964) and the work of Young and Willmott (1973). However, whilst Parsons's views concerning marital equality seem to be based on very little empirical evidence and therefore on blind faith in the 'system',[3] the other writers all discuss the social changes that in their opinion have led to the achievement of greater marital equality in Britain.

Fletcher and Young and Willmott place great emphasis on the role of the feminist movement and the abolition of formal barriers to sexual equality inside and outside marriage, economic growth and the decrease in the size of the average family since Victorian times. These are powerful arguments and there is no doubt that the position of women has improved considerably but, to paraphrase Gillespie (1971), more power does not mean equal power. The achievement of legal and political rights has not been matched by the equalisation of social conditions that is essential to the exercise of civil status. Consequently, 'public equality' coexists with 'private dependence' and the issue of sexual equality refuses to go away (Wainwright, 1978).

Although the work of Young and Willmott has already been mentioned critically in another context, the range and diversity of their research deserves special attention. From their earliest studies in the East End of London, they seem to have been committed to the view that marriage increasingly involves a 'partnership' in terms of the household division of labour and authority (Young and Willmott, 1962, pp. 25-30; Willmott and Young, 1967, p. 61; Willmott, 1969, p. 294). In fact, their more recent thesis concerning the growth of the symmetrical family was to a large extent expressed in embryo in Willmott's 1969 article (pp. 294-5):

The partnership takes three main forms. First it is a partnership in power, with major decisions being discussed and made jointly. Secondly, it is a partnership in the division of labour within the home, as the old distinctions between men's and women's jobs (though still made) become increasingly blurred . . . Thirdly, it is a partnership in social life, with couples spending more of their free time together and with their children. One could sum up by saying that, despite the inequalities that remain between the sexes, women now have higher status, and that there is a greater equality in society and in the family.

On the basis of studies undertaken over a number of years in Bethnal Green, 'Greenleigh' and Woodford, it is suggested that the 'shift towards the home and towards marriage partnership' has gone furthest among suburban middle-class couples and that the 'working-class are following the middle' (Willmott, 1969, p. 295). At the same time the possibility of exceptions that do not necessarily disprove the rule are noted, such as professional and managerial families. Four years later the term partnership is rejected in favour of the concept of symmetry, and the growth of partnership in marriage is now des-cribed as the growth of symmetry (Young and Willmott, 1973, p. 31-2). Despite the inclusion of additional exceptions to the trend, such as the old, the poor, shift-workers and managing directors, the same basic thesis is advanced.

Notwithstanding the fact that 'Power has not been distributed equally in more than a few families' (Young and Willmott, 1973, p. 31), the authors' confidence in the validity of their growth-of-symmetry thesis remains unshaken. Yet throughout their study they offer potential critics plenty of evidence and arguments with which to undermine their historical and class generalisations. In addition to the points made in Chapter 2 of the present study, it can also be noted that Young and Willmott concede that support from their own data for their interpretation of social change is weak in many instances—for example, in the key cases of the redistribution of income within the family and married women and work outside the home (ibid., pp. 82, 118). Another example concerns their material on leisure which provides considerable evidence of leisure inequalities, including one respondent who wrote in his diary: 'Made love every night. Pinned wife down and then went to bed' (ibid., p. 211). Yet another concerns the wives who first of all have to seek their husband's approval before they go out to work (ibid., pp. 101-2). Elsewhere they describe the extent to which shift-workers and managing directors subordinate their family life to work, although in the case of the former the detailed implications are not explored. In the case of the managing directors, a highly asymmetrical pattern emerges: 'the work always comes first. The family has to wait' is a typical quote from this part of their study (ibid., p. 251). Instead of revising their general theory, Young and Willmott proceed to dismiss this and other exceptions as minority patterns that will not, in their view, spread to other sections of society.

Young and Willmott have been heavily criticised by several commentators in Britain who in the main have not found it necessary to go beyond Young and Willmott's own contradictory evidence to establish the dubiousness of the 'growth of the symmetrical family' thesis. One such writer is Oakley (1974), who has attacked the study on methodological grounds, namely, that symmetry partly refers to housework, yet Young and Willmott only included one biased question on the division of labour in the home. Oakley concludes: 'Doubt is cast on the view that marriage is an egalitarian relationship' and 'There is a long way to go before equality even appears on the horizon' (1974, p. 164). Others have questioned the reliability and validity of Young and Willmott's study of the symmetrical family and have come to the conclusion that it is 'superficial' (Bell and Newby, 1976, p. 166) and 'profoundly unsociological' (Bell, 1974). Finally, the Young and Willmott argument that women's entry into the labour force leads to increasing sexual equality and sex role desegregation, and generally 'enhances' marital symmetry, has been critically evaluated by Wainwright (1978). She found that the distinctive character of female employment in contemporary Britain does not threaten, in a radical way, her traditional domestic role. Thus, the extent of job segregation by sex and the extent of various forms of sexual inequality would seem to be as widespread in industry as they are among the research families of the present study (Counter Information Services, 1976; Equal Opportunities Commission, 1978b).

The work of Blood and Wolfe (1960) in America is comparable in many ways to the most recent work of Young and Willmott (1973) in Britain. Both studies have utilised doubtful methods to advance highly contentious theses, which, in the case of Blood and Wolfe, involve the claim that patriarchy has given way to egalitarianism. More specifically, Safilios-Rothschild (1969) and Gillespie (1971) have shown that the measurement of marital power by Blood and Wolfe is biased in favour of egalitarianism. This is achieved by not weighting decisions in terms of 'importance' and/or discounting certain decisions quite arbitrarily from the analysis. The assumptions behind Blood and Wolfe's study have also been the subject of considerable criticism, especially by Gillespie, who argues that they assume the following: (1) that the husband can have power if he wants it, (2) that most couples start marriage as equals in terms of power and (3) that in the competition for the control of resources, husbands and wives are equal (1971, p. 448). The main thrust of Gillespie's evidence and analysis is that none of these assumptions holds in the case of married couples in America. What happens according to Gillespie is that men and women start off unequally and in the marital struggle for power women are consistently handicapped by a 'system of institutionalised male supremacy' and consequently 'Equal power women do not have' (1971, pp. 457-8).

In her study of conjugal role relationships, Bott is unusually reticent on the subject of conjugal power and authority. There is a fleeting reference to the coincidence of joint participation and joint decision-making, and mention of an 'ethic of equality' that pervades marriages organised on a joint basis (1971, pp. 52, 83, 95). However, there is no systematic discussion of the matter, which, in view of Bott's theory of the role of external sources of material and social support and the patterning of conjugal role relationships, is a strange omission. In the work of Blood and Wolfe (1960) and many other theorists,[4] such factors have been conceived in terms of an interpersonal resource theory of conjugal power and authority.

The case against the view that there has been a trend towards the equalisation of power within marriage can be said to revolve around the gap between the progressive implementation of formal measures designed to equalise sexual relationships in society and the failure to demonstrate conclusively that in practice sexual equality has been achieved either outside or inside marriage. In a review of the mainly American literature, Bernard has concluded that 'so far as the actual relations between husbands and wives are concerned, there has been no research proof that egalitarianism has been increasing' (1973, p. 127). In fact, Bernard was of the opinion that, if anything, the reverse was true and it was the husband's power that was increasing. Although not as plentiful, the evidence in Britain seems to point in the same direction. In addition to the work of Oakley (1974) and the exaggerated claims of Young and Willmott (1973) that have already been noted, one can search through the most recently published research papers and find little or no evidence to support the view that marriages today involve an equalisation of power (Barker and Allen, 1976a and 1976b). Instructively, in the Pahls' study of middle-class couples it was found that 'though all the sixteen couples said that any important decision would be discussed by both of them together, nine out of the sixteen agreed that the final decision was made by the husband' (1971, p. 213).

Following Safilios-Rothschild (1969), a wide range of decisions were investigated in the present study with the aid of questionnaires and interview data collected separately from each spouse. The perceived importance and frequency of each decision was noted, in addition to who had the most influence. In this way it was possible to construct a hierarchy of decisions in terms of 'importance' which 'correlated' rather well with who had most influence and the frequency of each decision.

The data presented in Table 5.1 could, on a simple numerical basis,

Table 5.1   *The Importance, Frequency and Pattern of Decision-Making in Different Areas of Family Life*

Decision area	Perceived importance	Frequency	Decision-maker (majority pattern)
Moving	Very important	Infrequent	Husband
Finance	Very important	Infrequent	Husband
Car	Important	Infrequent	Husband
House	Very important	Infrequent	Husband and wife
Children's education	Very important	Infrequent	Husband and wife
Holidays	Important	Infrequent	Husband and wife
Weekends	Not important	Frequent	Husband and wife
Other leisure activities	Not important	Frequent	Husband and wife
Furniture	Not important	Infrequent	Husband and wife
Interior decorations	Not important	Infrequent	Wife
Food and other domestic spending	Not important	Frequent	Wife
Children's clothes	Not important	Frequent	Wife

be interpreted as evidence of egalitarian decision-making among professional workers and their wives. After all, in exactly half of the decisions that are listed, a majority of both husbands and wives reported that the decisions were taken by them together. For example, what to do at weekends was reported as an equally shared decision by approximately 75 per cent of husbands and 70 per cent of wives, the same pattern was reported for holidays by 85 per cent of husbands and 75 per cent of wives, and the decision to buy new furniture was reported as an equal one by over 70 per cent of both husbands and wives. As far as decisions about children's education and selecting a new house were concerned, nearly every couple reported that these were equally shared decisions. The remaining non-egalitarian decisions were allocated equally to either the husband or the wife in most families. For instance, decisions regarding overall financial control were reported as being mainly or solely the responsibility of the husband by approximately 85 per cent of the husbands and over 70 per cent of the wives. The proportion of husbands and wives who reported husband domination in car-buying decisions and wife domination in the area of children's clothes were more or less the same, namely, 65 and 90 per cent respectively. At a glance, therefore, a spurious egalitarianism could be inferred, with some decisions being shared equally and the rest equally distributed between the husband and the wife in a majority of the families studied.

However, Table 5.1 suggests that, generally speaking, the more important though less frequent decisions tend to be husband-dominated, whereas the less important though more frequent decisions tend to be left to the wife. In between are a range of decisions that tend to be of varying importance and frequency, and these decisions were taken by spouses together in most cases. From the standpoint that not all family decisions are of equal importance, it can be shown that decision-making among professional workers and their wives is not egalitarian but husband-dominated. In other words, 'important' family decisions are either taken by the husband or by the husband and wife together; they are rarely taken by the wife alone in most professional families.

Among the research families there was a striking degree of consensus about what were 'important' decisions and what were not, and what constituted 'importance'. Basically, decisions that involved large sums of money were defined by all the research couples as either important or very important. Secondly, decisions that related to the husband's main role of breadwinner were defined as either important or very important, in contrast to decisions that related to the wife's main role of homemaker which tended to be defined as less important. This pattern of evaluation is of course entirely congruent with the tendency to label 'what women do as inferior to what men do' (Lopata, 1972, p. 363) and to trivialise the housework role (Oakley, 1976). This appeared to have been internalised by many of the wives and may well have contributed to a lack of confidence in their ability to take certain decisions. One of the many comments to this effect came from a wife who claimed:

> He makes the decisions, I gather the information. I don't want the responsibility of being wrong and decisions generally affect him more than me. My world is much smaller than his, so I always assume that he knows a great deal more about things than I do.

Decisions concerning money reflected very clearly the tendency to relegate the less important decisions to the wife. Typically, the husband decided the overall allocation of financial resources and had most say in the case of decisions involving large sums of money, whereas the wife in every research family tended to make all the 'minor' decisions. Interview data that illustrate the husband-dominant pattern in this contentious area of family life are presented below.

One has a family budget and a personal allowance out of it, including my own cheque book, but one still can't automatically spend ten pounds.   (Wife)

My husband decides the amount, and I spend it.   (Wife)

I've educated her. She has an allowance and budgets from that.
                                                              (Husband)

My husband doesn't always appreciate the rise in the cost of living. He can overspend but I can't.   (Wife)

He pays me monthly and I have to ask for a rise.   (Wife)

Husband says how much we have to spend [on holidays] and I organise it.   (Wife)

My husband has the final say because it is his money. I decide the actual spending.   (Wife)

The minor things to do with the house and children the wife decides.   (Husband)

He knows how much he has got in the bank and how much we can spend, so he decides. I get a fixed monthly allowance.   (Wife)

She gets a global sum each month and she decides how to spend it.   (Husband)

When the car needs something it has to have it, but when a wife needs something it doesn't because it is not a legal requirement.
                                                                 (Wife)

I wouldn't spend a lot without asking or saying, but the cost of living is going up all the time.   (Wife)

The interview data indicate that the main pattern was for the husband to 'give' his wife a regular sum of money and to have most say in the amount. Moreover, as a 'private' matter, there was no guarantee that the amount would be increased in line with the rate of inflation.[5] Consequently, the real extent of husband domination and wife dependence and subordination is revealed by a more detailed examination. In addition the perceived legitimacy and paternalism that attach to this and other 'important' areas of family life can be seen.

Decisions concerned with moving house, for example, when and where to, were regarded by every couple as extremely important and reported by every couple as husband-dominated. This area of decision-making was in fact discussed in Chapter 3 in the context of the general subordination of family life to the husband's work career. In a preliminary way it was suggested and demonstrated that to the extent that moving was associated with the husband's entry to the labour market, and subsequent movement within it, respondents considered it a 'career' decision. Once decisions relating to moving were defined in this way, it was widely regarded as entirely legitimate for the husband to have most say on the grounds that he was in the best position to judge the situation and/or that it affected him more than any other member of the family. Thus, in all the research families the location of the family home after marriage was determined by the location of the husband's work. And at the time of the fieldwork, only two couples out of a total of thirty-eight lived in the north-west of England for reasons not connected with the husband's work career. Significantly, however, in both these cases non-work career considerations had only been allowed to enter the decision-making process when the husband had defined the situation as one in which he was no longer concerned with career advancement.

The issue of moving from one region to another, or from one country to another, was discussed in some detail with each husband and below are some of the responses.

If it came to accepting a new job, I would have already sorted out my wife.   (Industrial Scientist)

I am prepared to move if the company request it. The family is important but I would firstly consider my position in the company.   (Industrial Scientist)

If my wife objected to moving I would try to persuade her and I think I would be successful.   (Industrial Scientist)

What is best for my family ... It is not entirely a career decision. At the moment though it is in my family's interests for me to advance my career as much as I can.   (Industrial Scientist)

For ten years we moved for my work. But last ten years have been stable for the wife and children's sake ... The main disagreement early in our marriage was leaving the wife's mother by herself and moving away. We moved back to the north-west at wife's request. Now that my career has peaked it doesn't matter so much, but

my career came first every move except the last one.
(Industrial Scientist)

The company asked me to move here. It was inconvenient domestically but good from a career point of view. I don't regret it . . . My
wife was not keen to move, she disliked the disruption and the loss
of friends and contacts.   (Industrial Scientist)

I was given four days' notice to join the new firm or be unemployed. She objected violently at the time, didn't want to move up
here. And we had to miss our annual holiday due to moving.
(Industrial Scientist)

I would override the wife's objections to moving, but would consider the children's education before deciding to make a move.
(Industrial Scientist)

Moved to the north-west for professional reasons first. I was
trained here, aware of the dental set-up at the hospital and had
many contacts here. Secondly, my mother, who was living on her
own, was up here.   (Dentist)

Some things are always sorted out beforehand. I would never apply
to go to a place Jane didn't want to go to. Anyway we would discuss
it first. We outwardly now get to the stage where we have to consider the children's education more than we used to, not very
seriously at the moment. The area is important too, job is more
important really. If the right job came along, this would overrule
everything.   (Academic)

These responses suggest that in the case of moves related to the husband's work career, the husband typically takes the final decision and
in taking that decision, the husband gives most consideration to his
work career. He occasionally takes into account the children's education, but rarely defers to his wife's objections. In many of the research
families, the wives did not object either to the husband making the
decision or to the decision itself: a clear indication of the extent of the
husband's legitimate domination in this crucial area of decision-
making. In those few instances in which the wives did object, they did
so for reasons connected with the disruption of their social lives and
work lives. For example, in research family no. 7, the wife regretted
moving because she had to give up work, in the knowledge that she
would be unable to get a similar post in the area of her husband's new
job. One or two other wives mentioned the possibility of their reduced

chances of promotion, especially wives who were teachers. But most of the wives studied, mentioned above all the many friends and neighbours (and sometimes relatives) they would miss due to moving. However, even the wives who claimed that they objected very strongly at the time of moving eventually acquiesced and commented that 'it was part of his job', or that it was 'good for him', or that 'if he is happy and interested, I don't mind' or equivalent sentiments.

Thus, in two of the most 'important' areas of family decision-making a picture of husband domination was consistently and emphatically reported. Among decisions that were shared, only two areas were perceived as 'very important'—housing and children's education. It is only as one progresses from the more to the less important areas of decision-making that one finds increasing evidence of wife domination. In other words, as far as decisions that were widely reported as 'very important' are concerned, the wife shared in two of them and was virtually excluded from the other two.

This pattern of husband domination among professional workers and their wives was confirmed in a variety of other ways. The value of interviewing husbands and wives separately was clearly illustrated by a comparison of couples' answers to various questions. Using this method it was sometimes possible to detect who was the most assertive during marital disagreements. For example, in research family no. 1, the wife said that she preferred holidays with her immediate family (of procreation). In her view such occasions provided an opportunity for her and her husband and child to spend some time together alone. However, during the interview with Mr Conner, he said that they spent every holiday with his parents.

Another example concerned research family no. 36. The husband explained that he chose his car and his wife's car and that she always accepted his decisions in these matters. Mrs Thompson mentioned to me separately that shopping in her new car was less enjoyable and more difficult now that she had a smaller car with only two doors. In fact she had not wanted to change her car. In the same family, the wife claimed that 'buying a house' was a 'joint and equal' decision; but the husband pointed out that he saw and bought their present house without his wife seeing it.

In research family no. 38, the wife said that she 'hated fast cars' and regarded them as a waste of money. The husband, however, enjoyed driving and owned a new, fast and expensive car. Finally, many wives reported that they disliked certain household tasks but conceded that their husbands did not 'help' with these particular tasks or generally as much as they would have liked. This often resulted in conflict, though rarely in the husband participating more in those tasks that he considered least satisfying or enjoyable; hence the noticeably higher rate of husband participation in child-care activities compared to domestic activities such as cleaning and ironing. In fact, in many respects the contrasting rates of husband participation in these two areas of activity reflect the husband's power to avoid legitimately, if he so wishes, those very tasks that he regards as most onerous.

The problem of not being able to persuade the husband to 'help' more in the home not only led to conflict and often defeat for the wife, it also had major implications for the way that she spent her time. In the case of married women who worked outside the home, this problem was acute even in families with paid domestic help. In this respect, the data from this study are no different from the survey findings from twelve countries showing that the working woman has less 'free' time than anyone else (Szalai, 1972, p. 119).

Marital conflict over what one respondent called 'demarcation disputes' (research family no. 24, husband) was far more frequently resolved in favour of the husband than the wife. The wives fell broadly into two approximately equal-sized groups; those who expressed satisfaction with their husband's level of domestic task participation and those who did not. The former group contained only full-time housewives whereas the latter group contained full-time housewives plus married women who worked either part-time or full-time outside the home. Both categories tended to talk in terms of 'my job' and 'his job', that is, domestic work and non-domestic work. A typical example of a wife who worked part-time and who was less than enthusiastic about doing virtually all the housework was Mrs Thompson (research family no. 36):

> As a matter of course, he doesn't do any housework, unfortunately. [Would you like him to?] Oh yes, anyone can do it as far as I am concerned. Well I suppose I wouldn't expect John to put an apron on and dash around with the hoover unless I was ill or something. A wife's work is to look after one's family, feeding, clothing, keeping clean and tidy. I would like him to, and he does help with the children a lot. But I wouldn't expect him to stay in and do the housework while I went out to work. Somehow this would be the wrong way round. But again, probably the way I've been brought up. My father [who was a general medical practitioner] never had time, never at home. John works very hard [as a dentist], I would not expect him to come home and do anything in the house.

Once again the allusion to the husband's work role legitimates his abstention from certain domestic tasks. Another example concerns research family no. 31; the wife had noted in her separate interview that her husband did not 'help' enough in the house, and the husband confirmed the situation:

> I've got a masculine attitude I suppose, in that I expect my meal to be ready when I come in. She does all the work and I lie around. This causes friction. I do some things and try and help out a little.

The wife did not work outside the home and did not expect a great deal of help from her husband, and, as the following extracts from the wife's interview reveal, did not receive it.

> I get annoyed with Richard because he watches the television a lot and I think he should be helping me to wash the dishes. He says watching the TV is relaxing after using his brain all day [the husband is an academic]. This gets me cross. Also reading the papers; he reads them all from cover to cover all day on Sunday and I really get annoyed about it . . . When you have got two young babies as I have, a little extra help is required, not necessarily scrubbing floors or washing dishes. But I think a husband should realise that it is quite tedious having two babies screaming all day and then expect me to be lively and happy when he comes home at night . . . He should help more at certain times of the month and then when the tension has gone, I'm quite prepared to do everything.

The extent to which many of the wives complained in vain about the household division of labour is perhaps a good indication of their relative powerlessness. Bott has warned about confusing male authoritarianism with conjugal role segregation (1971, p. 64), but it seems likely that dissatisfaction with a highly segregated conjugal role structure is more widespread among wives than husbands, and such a pattern, like the complaints associated with it, is often a fair reflection of the husband's power.

The husband has a major influence over some of the crucial decisions affecting where the wife's domestic role is to be performed, under what circumstances, and often whether or not it is going to be a full- or part-time activity. It was also evident that the wives of professional workers were in a relatively powerless position in relation to the impact of their husband's work schedule on their daily lives. Many wives resented not knowing when the husband would be arriving home for dinner and the husband's intermittent and often unpredictable absence from home due to conferences, business trips or simply working late. Some of the relevant data pertaining to this general issue have already been quoted in an earlier chapter. The following extracts from the separate interviews with the wives are therefore supplementary.

The only thing I don't like about the day is having to get the meal at night. I never know what time he is coming in, it might be any time between 5 and 7 p.m. and that chunk of my day is taken away. (Academic's Wife)

Last year he went away for two weeks in December, a bit much here on my own. But it is a good break for him, takes him away from the routine, as it were . . . I don't sleep very well on my own . . . I don't mind him working at home, I feel he must do this anyway. (Industrial Scientist's Wife)

[Object to husband's absence?] No, not now. I did to start with. Anyway I've got a career, I belong to a professional association. I never go because unfortunately they are on the night Jim goes out to squash. (Dentist's Wife)

He goes [away to conferences] and that's all right so long as it doesn't happen to be at a time when it's terribly inconvenient. But if I want to get away and I have to look after the children, I get a bit fed up. (Academic's Wife)

Sometimes the husbands commented on their wives' objections regarding the extent to which their work influenced the pattern of family life:

I haven't asked my wife if she minds, something that just happens. (Industrial Scientist)

I've always studied at home, she was conditioned to it from the start. (Academic)

The evidence seems to suggest that the intrusion of the husband's work activities on family life was not a 'problem' as far as the husbands were concerned; it was only a problem for their wives.

However, the husband's work career was not the only constraint on the housewife's autonomy. As Oakley (1974) has pointed out, responsibility for the home and the children also considerably limits the housewife's freedom of movement and activities. Wives with preschool children were especially restricted by the need to feed and generally care for them and by the work they generate. Consequently, it is difficult to disagree with Oakley when she notes that 'In the housewife's case autonomy is more theoretical than real' (1974, p. 43), although it may be necessary to qualify this statement by reference to the stage in the family life-cycle. Autonomy is possibly greater among 'middle-class' housewives who are near or at the post-parental stage of the family life-cycle than it is among young and particularly 'working-class' housewives (Gavron, 1966; Oakley, 1974).

Throughout this analysis of conjugal power and authority, it has been apparent that the wives' comments indicated a much lower level of self-esteem than did the husband's comments. Many of the wives regarded housework as boring and by implication regarded themselves as boring and uninteresting people. During the course of discussing the issue of decision-making in general terms it came as no surprise to find that among a majority of the research couples the husbands were far more self-confident and assertive than the wives, who correspondingly tended to be more passive and prepared to take a subservient position.

I prefer to rely on my husband as he has more confidence to make decisions. (Wife)

In theory we take decisions as a family, have a vote on it. And my vote has a little more weight than others. (Husband)

I am prepared to be convinced by my husband. (Wife)

I never decide anything without consulting her, ever. But I usually decide. (Husband)

It suits me to have decisions made for me. I'm not a decision-maker. (Wife)

Wife thinks I should decide anyway. She worries about taking away my power of deciding. (Husband)

Basically I feel I like to be dominated, although I like to be consulted in decisions. (Wife)

By and large I decide nearly everything. Everything that matters I decide. I do consult my wife and she always agrees with me. (Husband)

Wives do not like making decisions. (Husband)

He does tend to make decisions then tell me, which I do not always like. I would prefer to talk about it first. (Wife)

I would not decide without consulting my wife, but maintain chairman's prerogative of the casting vote. (Husband)

Men have to be the main decision-makers to survive. Therefore in complete equality they would lose their masculinity. I would not want this.   (Wife)

Wives look to their husbands as being the leader, the man of the house, being in charge.   (Wife)

Women generally like to be 'managed' by men. This is instinctive. You can't have two bosses in the home. A woman 'bossing' a man is, to me, unnatural.   (Husband)

I would still expect the father to be the ultimate authority in the family . . . I don't really care much for domineering wives.   (Wife)

Finally, one husband talked in terms of having the ability to 'veto' certain decisions and his wife not having a 'veto' on anything. At the very least, this material and the data quoted elsewhere indicate the extent to which most of the research couples accepted the subordination of wives and the superordination of husbands as natural and expedient. It also confirms the view that the marital relationship is very much a 'deferential one in that it is traditionally-legitimated and hierarchical' (Bell and Newby, 1976b, p. 164). In contrast to certain optimistic social theorists who claim that the nineteenth-century patriarchal family has been superseded by a more 'democratic' type (Blood and Wolfe, 1960; Fletcher, 1962; Burgess, Locke and Thomes, 1962; Young and Willmott, 1973), the present study provides abundant evidence of the survival of patriarchalism. The research couples legitimated their patriarchal attitudes and practices with reference to custom, biology and sometimes the greater knowledge and involvement of the husband in the more 'important' areas of family life.

Overall, therefore, there was a tendency to continue to associate the husband-provider role with the power of decision-making and the role of the housewife, part- or full-time, with passivity and dependence. This was implied in much of the data collected from both husbands and wives and none more so than the wife who described conjugal roles in the following terms:

Men should be the mainstay of the household, should be able to lean on one's husband. There are certain tasks which you know one regards as masculine and which he should fulfil willingly and competently. In the main, being the breadwinner, unless it is not possible through illness. Taking the responsibility in making the decisions, probably supporting one's wife in any problems or anything. [Wife?] She should be a complement to him. Look after all the domestic arrangements with a little help with the dishes, and deal with the minor problems with regard to the children.

(Industrial Scientist's Wife)

Husband dominance was also clearly indicated during the joint interview. On most occasions it was the husband who presumed to speak for himself and his wife, rarely did the wife presume to speak for her husband. For example, in answer to the question on the possibility of winning or inheriting a large sum of money, in twenty-one cases both the husband and wife responded, in fifteen cases the husband spoke on behalf of his wife who was present at the time, and two husbands replied on behalf of their absent wives. In response to this particular question not one wife presumed to speak on behalf of her husband.

Cumulatively, therefore, the many different 'slices of data' (Glaser and Strauss, 1968) tend to point in the same direction, namely, that among professional workers and their wives at the child-rearing stage of the family cycle it is the husband who wields most power.[6] To a large extent, the power to control one's own life and the lives of others, even against their will, accrues 'automatically' to the husband-breadwinner. The tendency to regard the husband's power in certain crucial areas of family life as legitimate merely transforms it into authority. Thus, the evidence from this study fully endorses Ralph Turner's view (1970, p. 263):

Determination of family decisions by outside events introduces an area of de facto decision making into the family. But the de facto decisions come by way of the husband, so that from the internal perspective of the family, there is automatic dominance by the husband in many decisions . . .

The husband is able to commit the family to a de facto decision or impose a decision to which other family members must make accommodation, because he is accorded the authority to dictate such decisions. Authority resides in acceptance by the family of the principle that exigencies of work life take priority and that the worker is the legitimate conveyor and interpreter of these demands from outside the group by way of a legitimate agent of the outside unit who is also a member of the group. Most of what we know as authority is of this character.

Thus, the combination of the relatively permanent, full-time presence of the husband/father in the economic division of labour outside the home, plus the tendency for the wife/mother to be mainly responsible for the home and children, irrespective of whether or not she participates in income-producing economic activity, seems to be the origin of the process that leads to husband domination. Once this pattern of sex role differentiation has been established and is widely supported ideologically, the socioeconomic dependence of married women on their husbands is virtually assured. Among the research couples, certain fundamental decisions, such as where the couple live, how often they move, the amount and redistribution of family income, the scheduling of family activities and the use of the wife's time, were all influenced directly or indirectly by the husband's greater involvement in and economic rewards from income-producing work. Significantly, a reduction in the impact of the husband's occupational career on family life was achieved in two of the families studied only when the husband concerned relaxed his career ambitions; in other words, when the husband's definition of the situation had changed.

Support for an emphasis on the economic basis of marriage and marital power comes from a variety of sources but especially from studies which show that when a wife goes out to work, her authority in the family tends to increase (Nye and Hoffman, 1965; Safilios-Rothschild, 1970a) and research which shows that 'the higher the husband's occupational prestige, the greater his voice in marital decisions' (Blood and Wolfe, 1960). However, this is not to deny the relevance of non-economic factors. Nevertheless the present study underlines the importance of a hierarchy of dependence in which the wife is economically dependent (subordinate) to her husband, who in turn is economically dependent (subordinate) upon income-producing work. Generally one finds that husbands have to 'accommodate' to work (Presthus, 1962) and wives to their husbands (Holmstrom, 1972). Familiarity with and awareness of this structure of relationships had led many research couples to regard it as unalterable and to proceed on this basis. It is in this context that sex role socialisation practices and beliefs, and sex role behaviour and norms that appear to reinforce the existing hierarchy of dependence, need to be understood.

Notes: Chapter 5

1 Extensive bibliographies, though in the main American, can be found in Bernard (1973) and Cromwell and Olson (1975). The best cross-cultural review of the relevant literature is by Goode (1970). For the 'radical' sources, the bibliography compiled by Rowbotham (1972) is indispensable.
2 The references mentioned under each heading are in no way meant to be exhaustive.
3 Writing from the perspective of a more wide-ranging critical review of Parsons's contribution to the sociology of the family, Morgan has stated that 'Parsons' account is permeated with an overall optimism and faith in the American system' and his work 'is largely an imaginative reconstruction and typification based upon the author's own participation in and membership of the system which he is describing' (1975, pp. 47, 62).

4 As already indicated, Gillespie (1971) is highly critical of this kind of theory on the grounds that it is excessively individualistic. Safilios-Rothschild (1976) has also criticised it as being 'a limited and inadequate derivative' of exchange theory that has tended to ignore the 'cost' associated with the supply and withdrawal of 'resources'.

5 According to a report in the *Guardian* (17 September 1975) two separate consumer surveys showed that 20 and 28 per cent of husbands respectively had not increased the housekeeping to their wives during the previous year.

6 A minor exception, apart from those already discussed, concerns the resolution of marital conflict in sexual matters. In this small-scale study over 70 per cent of husbands and wives reported that sexual disagreements were settled by 'mutual consent', six wives and five husbands reported that the 'husband gave in' and two wives and four husbands reported that the 'wife gave in'.

CHAPTER 6

The Leisure Patterns of Professional Workers and Their Wives

Throughout the previous analysis the distinction between paid work and domestic work inside the home has figured prominently. The tendency for husbands to be mainly responsible for the first kind and for wives to be mainly responsible for the second kind of work has been shown to be crucial to the patterning of household tasks, child-care activities and marital power and authority among professional couples. In this chapter it will be argued that the distinction between the two types of work and their association with a particular sex is equally relevant when considering leisure.

Work and leisure

One of the major problems in studying leisure has been the development of an adequate definition (Rapoport and Rapoport, 1974), and one of the most common solutions has been to define it in relation to work (Parker, 1972). Initially, leisure can be defined as time spent on activities by an individual after he/she has undertaken all his/her work and family obligations. In fact definitions of this kind have a long tradition in sociology. For example, Veblen in his classic study of the status and functions of leisure suggested that the 'characteristic feature of leisure class life is a conspicuous exemption from all useful employment' (Veblen, 1970, p. 44). More recently, the tendency to define leisure in relation to work and to focus one's interest on both has been a prominent feature of research in this area.[1]

One of the most comprehensive and widely quoted attempts to examine leisure in relation to work is Parker's 'three typical ways in which people tend to relate their work to their leisure' (Parker, 1971, p. 180).

Briefly, the extension pattern consists of having leisure activities which are often similar in content to one's working activities and of making no sharp distinction between what is considered as work and what is leisure. With the opposition pattern leisure activities are deliberately unlike work and there is a sharp distinction between what is work and what is leisure. Finally, the neutrality pattern consists of having leisure activities which are generally different from work but not deliberately so, and of appreciating the difference between work and leisure without always defining the one as the absence of the other. (Parker, 1972, pp. 101-2).

Parker analyses these three work-leisure patterns mainly from the point of view of the individual. In a later publication he states that they are 'offered as systematic explanations of differences found in the work and leisure behaviour and attitudes of individuals and groups' and 'should be thought of as tendencies and probabilities rather than as rigid categories' (Parker, 1973, p. 77).

Notwithstanding the tentative nature of Parker's theory, his typology is susceptible to criticism. First, it excludes all those adults who do not work full-time outside the home, for example, the unemployed, the elderly and housewives. Secondly, Parker's theory tends to assume that in general professional/managerial occupations involve a 'positive' relationship to work and that manual occupations involve a 'negative' attachment to work. The possibilities that a professional worker can experience work as an 'alienating' and 'damaging' activity, and that a manual worker can experience work as 'creative' and 'fulfilling' activity, are not allowed for in Parker's typology. Thirdly, Parker's theory tends to gloss over the class and therefore the unequal and contradictory character of leisure in modern society. For instance, the emergence of leisure as a product that is exchanged in the market place, just like any other scarce commodity, has meant that there are those with plenty of time but who lack economic resources with which to purchase certain leisure products. On the other hand, there are those who have considerable economic resources but tend to be short of time, although the claim that 'professional and business employees have less leisure time than the mass of clerical and manual workers' (Parker, 1972, p. 180) is probably exaggerated. This is mainly because such comparisons tend to be based on the number of hours worked each week rather than the number of weeks worked each year (Young and Willmott, 1973).

Perhaps the most pertinent criticism of Parker, as far as this study is concerned, is the sexism that is implicit in his approach. In Parker's various expositions of his work and leisure theory, women are briefly and infrequently mentioned (Parker, 1971, pp. 178-81; 1972, pp. 29-30; 1973, pp. 75-7; 1976, pp. 86-8), and on each occasion women are either discussed in the context of 'minority' groups of 'non-workers' (such as 'prisoners' and the 'unemployed'), or are relegated to a section under the heading 'the family'. Consequently, Parker tends systematically to exclude women from his analysis of work and leisure and similarly to exclude men from his analysis of leisure and the family. In effect, Parker assumes that all men are workers and all women are housewives; though he is never explicit for he uses the term 'people' when he really means 'men' (for example, Parker, 1976, pp. 72-3) and the term 'housewife' to refer to all women (for example, Parker, 1972, p. 30). As a result of his androcentric approach, which is of course far from unique in sociology (Oakley, 1974, pp. 1-28), Parker is quite unable to comprehend the role of men as husbands and fathers in relation to leisure, or the role of women as workers and/or domestic workers in relation to leisure. To paraphrase Oakley, women are 'invisible' in the sociology of leisure except in their role as housewives.

In order to build upon Parker's 'first faltering steps towards an adequate theory of work-leisure relationships' (Parker, 1973, p. 75) it is imperative to recognise first that domestic work is work and to investigate the extent of male and female participation in such work, and secondly, to recognise that women as well as men go out to work, and to examine the incidence and type of paid employment among men and women. Thus, following Veblen (1970), DeGrazia (1962), Dumazedier (1967), Parker (1972), and many others, it is possible to distinguish between different 'components of life space' (Parker, 1972, p. 25) and at the same time incorporate the notion of domestic work as work. Therefore, apart from attending to one's physiological needs, an individual's life space can be divided into three categories: work (and work obligations), domestic work (and domestic work obligations) and leisure. The exclusion of work obligations, domestic or otherwise, from the category leisure indicates that many activities are of a preparatory kind and although they may be experienced as enjoyable, they do not express what many regard as the essential quality of leisure, namely, its discretionary character.

In all categories of life space there are two key dimensions, time and activity (Parker, 1972, p. 27), both of which are sensitive to the availability of economic resources. Consequently, one cannot divorce the study of leisure from the distribution of resources and therefore from the distribution of power over resources in society and the family. This point was thoroughly appreciated by Veblen who defined leisure as the 'non-productive consumption of time' (1970, p. 46) and suggested that the emergence of a non-productive leisure class was historically dependent upon the prior existence of an economic surplus and the concomitant differentiation of society into those who were engaged in productive labour and those who were not. Both work and domestic work are 'productive' in the Veblenian sense of being motivated and characterised by the welfare of the group; in Veblen's own words, by serviceability or workmanship. Thus, for Veblen, pecuniary strength was fundamental to the availability of leisure time and the selection of leisure activities. By contrast, the contemporary focus on leisure as 'free choice', 'choosing time', and so on, is in danger of overlooking the political economy of leisure time and leisure activities; that is, the influence of the production and distribution of wealth on leisure. This oversight can take the form of neglecting the structured inequality of leisure opportunities and experiences,[2] or it can take the form of assuming that 'leisure' has in some way been 'democratised'.[3] Above all, therefore, this chapter will be concerned with leisure inequalities between and within the research families.

Leisure patterns

In general terms, among professional workers and their wives at the child-rearing stage of the family cycle there was a tendency for the amount of time devoted to leisure to increase with age. In the light of this pattern, the research families were allocated to one of three groups based on a combination of work and family careers: (1) early work and family career couples (eleven); (2) mid-work and family career couples (thirteen); (3) late work and family career couples (fourteen).[4] However, in addition to the broad relationship between leisure time and career stage, there were marked differences between husbands and wives with respect to both the availability of leisure time and type of leisure activity.

Early work and family career couples

The work and family career circumstances of this group seemed to combine to limit severely the availability of leisure time to both husbands and wives. Every research couple in this 'establishment phase' (Rapoport and Rapoport, 1975) were at the beginning of the process of buying their own house, furnishing, decorating and often altering it and their garden. This stage was also typically one in which the wife ceased to work outside the house in order to care for young children. The husband was at a relatively low point of his work-life income profile (Glick and Parke, 1965; Bell, 1971). In the absence of financial and domestic services from kin, the simultaneous decline in income and increase in family expenditure and domestic work obligations seems to result in a marked decline in the time available for leisure among couples at this work and career stage. In addition, the situation was often exacerbated by the relatively greater opportunities for career advancement that by definition exist at the lower levels of a bureaucratic career. Consequently, during this early career stage, faced with expanding financial commitments and the absence of a second income (the wife's), husbands tended to be highly aspirant in their work careers and to be prepared to work long hours, and migrate to improve their work and market situation. The data on migration showed that this was a far more frequent event during this work and family career stage than at any other. Finally, if a couple spaced their children with a thought to the wife returning to work at the earliest possible moment, the time available for leisure was further reduced.

This pattern of a shortage of leisure time among the early work and career stage couples was very much in evidence as can be seen from the following case studies. The Holdens (research family no. 5) had been married four years and had one child under a year old. They had recently moved to the area to improve Mr Holden's salary and future career prospects and started to buy their first house. The Holdens spent a lot of their time on their new house and garden and said that most weekday evenings Mrs Holden 'did sewing and mending' or helped Mr Holden with the garden or more usually the decorating. The weekends were the same; as far as Mr Holden was concerned, they represented a 'chance to do some work on the house'. The Holdens claimed that they enjoyed all these home improvement activities but emphasised that it was 'cheaper to do it ourselves'. Mr Holden explained how he was trying to advance his career as fast as he could because 'right now' this was in the 'best interests' of his immediate family. To this end, he often worked late and was prepared to go away on business trips at his employer's request. Mrs Holden noted that 'they used to do a lot more, especially together, but there was no time these days with a baby and a house to cope with'. Throughout the joint interview, Mr and Mrs Holden repeatedly mentioned examples of leisure interests and activities that had declined with the advent of marriage, a family and moving; 'we like walking but don't do much now', 'used to go to church regularly, have been very lazy recently', 'used to read a lot, not time for much now'. The Holdens were fairly typical of the early work and family career stage couples in their isolation from kin services, the amount of time they spent on their new house, garden and growing family, and in the ways in which Mr Holden was responding to the situation both at work and at home.

Another research couple who illustrated the extent of the demands upon their time during this career stage were the Owens (research family no. 29). The Owens had two pre-school children and had been living in the area for just over one year. Mr Owen stated that most of his time in the evenings and at weekends was taken up with work-related obligations such as preparing lecture courses for his new job and papers for publication. The Owens frequently alluded to their relative poverty, their lack of nearby kin to help with the children and the innumerable ways in which having two young children affected their lives. For example, Mrs Owen said that earlier in their marriage, when she had worked as a teacher, they could afford to go out in the evenings and that she had the time to do voluntary youth work: 'I used to do a lot of youth work while I was teaching, but I haven't since the children came along.' In Mrs Owen's view, such activities were 'impossible with young children'. For his part, Mr Owen noted that Mrs Owen was reluctant to leave the children 'with someone who doesn't know them very well'. He said that when he was not at the university he divided his time between preparation for work, the house and his wife and children. As far as the Owens were concerned, when their work and domestic work obligations were fulfilled there was little time, money or 'energy' left over for anything else.

A comparable work, family and leisure pattern occurred in another academic family (research family no. 30). The Parkers had returned from abroad five years previously and had two pre-school children. Mr Parker was currently writing up his thesis, and as a result 'for the past year our social life had been nil', said Mrs Parker. At this point in the joint interview, Mr Parker explained that this situation was also due 'partly to having very young children, which take up a lot of your [that is, the wife's] energy'. Mrs Parker then added that it 'has been a busy four years having children and setting up home here, and all our old friends have moved away'. Once again the combination of work and domestic work role obligations during this early career stage seemed to be largely responsible for the marked and widely regretted shortage of leisure time.

Perhaps the most extreme case among the research couples at this career stage were Mr and Mrs Harding (research family no. 19). The Hardings had one child aged 3 years and, owing to the pressure of their financial situation, Mrs Harding continued to work outside the home after the birth of their child. Without kin aid of any kind and with a new and large mortgage to repay, Mr and Mrs Harding both emphasised the lack of leisure time in their current situation. They described how every weekday evening Mr Harding collected their child from the nursery and Mrs Harding returned home direct from work to prepare the evening meal. After dinner, Mrs Harding 'gets him to bed while I wash up', explained Mr Harding. Most evenings the Hardings were engaged in various activities in and around the house and garden. Typically Mrs Harding did housework, sewed and knitted, whereas Mr Harding decorated and did gardening. In the case of the Hardings the scarcity of time and money seemed to have heightened the marital struggle for leisure. Mrs Harding noted that all her leisure activities at the moment were connected to the home. This was in contrast to Mr Harding who went out with friends to play sport and have a drink every Friday evening while his wife organised the washing. On Saturday afternoon, Mrs Harding usually did the ironing and other similar domestic chores while Mr Harding watched sport on the television. This whole topic was a major source of conflict, and although Mr Harding emphasised that he did his '50 per cent' of the housework, it was apparent from the interview data that Mrs Harding had far less time for leisure than her husband.

In the case of the non-bureaucratically employed professional worker and his wife, the leisure pattern during this early career stage was similar to the salaried couples. Thus it was still the wife who specialised in a home role and the husband who was more preoccupied with a work career outside the home. Like the industrial scientists and academics, dentists reported considerable 'overtime' on such things as accounts, journals and attendance at courses and professional association meetings. Despite evidence of greater affluence in the form of larger and more lavishly equipped houses, the early career dentists consistently mentioned the problem of time, and especially the piece-work basis of dentistry which meant that if they took time off from work, they did not earn any money.

In general, therefore, early career couples tended to experience a marked decline of both leisure time and activities compared to earlier in their lives. This characteristic shortage of leisure time and the change to more 'work'-related 'leisure' activities could be termed an 'extension leisure pattern' (Parker, 1972). However, such a description tends to conceal the extent to which leisure time contracts during this early work and family career stage. Secondly, although the term certainly applies to both husbands and wives, it also fails to reveal the fact that it is easier for the husband to 'escape' from his work than it is for the wife to 'escape' from her domestic work (Gavron, 1966; Hobson, 1978). Thus, whilst Oakley (1974) has highlighted the significance of the separation of the world of work and the private world of the home and the designation of these spheres to men and women respectively, for the isolated housewife this division is also important from the standpoint of leisure. The lack of any physical or temporal boundary between work and non-work seemed to result in the wives 'working' longer hours and having fewer leisure interests and activities that were quite unconnected with their primary role responsibilities, compared to their husbands. The wives at this stage and the later stages invariably included among their leisure activities tasks that were elaborations of their domestic role, for instance, cooking, sewing, knitting and reading about these activities. For one wife (research family no. 14), the problem of transcending the domestic role 'extended' to holidays: 'Sometimes I think I just take my ordinary housework somewhere else.'

Mid-work and family career couples

The major changes in the circumstances of professional workers and their wives at this stage mainly concern the ages of the children and by implication the time resources of the wife. When the children are all at school, it is the wife who tends to gain most from the altered time schedule of family activities. This is especially the case if the wife does not return to employment outside the home. In other words, once it has been shown that it is the wife who participates most in domestic and child-care tasks, the daily absence of children and the work they create benefits the wife's life-style noticeably more than the husband's. At the same time the incidence of migration every few years in search of an improved career position starts to slow down during this stage, as many husbands begin to approach the peak of their careers. They tend also to become more willing to forfeit the possibility of promotion for what they often described as 'the sake of the children's education'. Also the husband's income by mid-career has usually risen considerably, due to annual increments and promotion in the case of bureaucratically employed professional workers, and due to increased proficiency and expansion of the practice in the case of independent professional workers. Thus, a combination of factors begins to operate at this stage and leads to an increase in the availability of leisure time. This is particularly marked for the wife on weekdays.

A good illustration of this change concerned research family no. 22. Mrs Field was the wife of an industrial scientist and they had two school-age children. For the past ten years they had been residentially stable, apart from a one-year assignment abroad when the children were much younger. During this whole period the Fields, and especially Mrs Field, developed extensive leisure interests and social relationships in the neighbourhood. Mrs Field was involved in a variety of musical activities, including playing, singing, dancing and listening. Although all the family were active in these pursuits, Mr Field was restricted by his work career and its demands, and the children by their schoolwork. Consequently, it was only Mrs Field who had the time to devote the majority of her life space to her many leisure interests.

As in the case of many of the research couples, time was a resource that was thought to be in short supply. Certainly, Mr and Mrs Field were acutely aware of the problem: 'The thing we are short of is time not money... Time is more important to us than money... wife cannot spare me more time, her time is filled already... If she went out to work we would have more cash maybe, but what we would lose would be time.' Mrs Field concurred with Mr Field's appraisal of the situation and expressed no wish to return to work (Mrs Field was a scientist). In her own words: 'I have so many interests that I have no

desire or time to return [to work] at the moment.' Later on Mrs Field
referred again to the same topic: 'I don't miss a career, I'm so
involved in things I'm interested in, I don't feel the need for a career.'

Not all the mid-career couples demonstrated the trend towards an
increase in leisure time to the same extent as the Fields. Those couples
who did not fully conform to this trend provided evidence of the
continuing influence of factors more commonly associated with the
first work and family career stage. If, for example, the couple moved,
or had additional children, or if the wife returned to work outside the
home, then the tendency to experience an increase in the availability of
leisure time was correspondingly reduced. Among the thirteen
research couples at this second career stage, two had recently moved,
in two other cases the wife had returned to part-time work outside the
home, and one couple had another child after their first two children
started school.

However, leisure is not just about time, it is also about choices, and
in this respect all the mid-career couples massively reflected the
presence of children in their leisure activities. Couple after couple
reported evenings and weekends spent on 'organising', 'helping' or
'supervising' their children's homework, and adult-sponsored leisure
activities such as music lessons, cubs, brownies, swimming and a
multiplicity of other sports and hobbies. Sometimes the parents
reported that they also participated in these organised activities, and
at other times they merely provided a 'ferry' service for the children.
Either way a considerable amount of leisure time was consumed by
husbands and wives in child-oriented behaviour. For example, Mr
Bond (research family no. 10) said that at weekends he and his wife
took their children swimming or rambling, or to places of interest that
were 'beneficial for children' such as museums and art galleries. One
husband (research family no. 15) went as far as to distinguish between
leisure activities that he would choose as an adult and those participated in as a parent: 'Any activities that we take up they [the children]
would have to participate in. Leisure pursuits tend to be ones that they
enjoy rather than ones that we would take up.'

This mid-career pattern of child-oriented 'leisure' time reinforced
the impression that it was the full-time housewife who tended to
benefit most from the increase in the availability of leisure time
associated with this stage, though not all the full-time, mid-career
housewives used their extra (day) time to develop interests beyond
those that were extensions of their primary role as homemaker. Some,
like Mrs Roberts (research family no. 33), were particularly isolated
and bound up with the domestic role. Mrs Roberts regretted that she
and her husband rarely went out together. This was because Mr
Roberts preferred to stay at home and relax after a long day in the

surgery. Mrs Roberts reported that she had one friend whom she occasionally accompanied to the theatre or cinema. Her other leisure activities were watching television, playing with her children and taking the dog out for a long walk each day, 'weather permitting'. Both Mr and Mrs Roberts claimed that their children were their major 'leisure interest', in fact Mrs Roberts said that she spent most of her free time 'playing games with the children'.

Thus, even during mid-career when the opportunities for increased leisure improve, some couples embraced their work and family roles so completely that they failed to develop new or take up old leisure interests. Instead, most of their leisure interests and activities were extensions of their primary roles as workers, domestic workers and parents. Generally, however, this mid-career stage is a period that is characterised by a marked decline in the wife's daytime workload, a decline in the husband's interest in his work career, expanding family income and an increase in the availability of leisure time. At weekends and during the evenings it was the wife's leisure time that was at a premium not her husband's, irrespective of whether or not she also worked outside the home. The wife's primary responsibility for the domestic work, plus the endless and ever-present nature of that work, combined to consistently erode the wife's leisure time and constrain her leisure interests and activities at this and at other career stages.

Late work and family career couples

Having regard to the main forces that influence the amount of leisure time available to professional workers and their wives, namely, work and domestic work and their related obligations, plus financial circumstances, one would expect that the late career stage would be typically characterised by a decline in the first two factors and an improvement in the third. From the data on professional couples at this stage, this seemed to be the case. The result once again was an increase in the leisure time available to husbands and wives, especially the latter. Therefore at this final parental stage the trend observable during the previous stage seems to accelerate in line with the further development of ongoing changes in a couple's socioeconomic circumstances. In other words, the husband typically experiences a further decline in his level of work career involvement. The wife's domestic workload may also decline as the children mature and require less attention, and/or as a result of employing a domestic worker. The cost of and dependence upon babysitting services may also cease to be a handicap. A familiar sentiment among the late career couples was 'now the children are older we can go out together again'.

Mr and Mrs Dyer (research family no. 13) conformed to this pattern well. Their list of leisure interests and activities was one of the longest in the sample. It included travel, learning languages, current affairs, sailing, climbing, walking, reading, entertaining, gardening and music, plus the usual home-decorating, cooking, making clothes and curtains, and so on. Holidays were particularly important to this couple. In the main they spent them with old friends and relatives abroad, and talked most enthusiastically about such occasions and how they wished they could spend more time on holiday. Mr and Mrs Dyer had two teenage sons and Mrs Dyer was a full-time housewife who also had domestic help.

Another late career couple who were similarly placed with regard to work and domestic work obligations were Mr and Mrs Price (research family no. 20). The Prices' leisure pursuits ranged from sports to participation in charitable organisations and the theatre. Mr Price was keen on 'do-it-yourself' and Mrs Price collected and swopped recipes and generally enjoyed culinary activities. The Prices were particularly sensitive to the likely effect of changes in their family situation on leisure time. They spoke of 'radical changes' in the future when their two teenage sons left home; of being alone; of all the extra time they would have and the need to 'become more involved in activities'. Mr Price (who was the dominant partner during the joint interview) summed up the situation in the following way: 'Let's be in on the organisation of the thing. Feel we are going to have to do something like that, because there will be more time available to us. In the past too I was away frequently, away from the home in London or abroad. That has died down a bit now.'

Mr and Mrs Price also compared their leisure pattern in the past with their current situation. For example, Mrs Price noted that earlier in the marriage they used to go out about 'once a week'. Now it was 'much more'. Mr Price mentioned that he was 'not so dedicated that I wouldn't like an extra day at the weekend'. As far as bringing work home was concerned, 'it happens far less now than it used to'. Thus, Mr and Mrs Price are a clear case of a late career couple who are experiencing an expansion of their leisure time due to a combination of work and family career changes.

However, if late career couples have a large number of children or space their children out over a long period, or if the wife returns to work outside the home, or if both spouses are in other respects highly identified with their work and family roles, it is unlikely that an increase in leisure time transpires. Mr and Mrs Kelly were such a family (research family no. 35). They had seven children who all lived at home and were aged between 9 and 21. For Mrs Kelly, domestic responsibility for a large house and family tended to leave very little time for leisure interests and activities outside the home. For Mr Kelly, high domestic expenses meant long working hours as a dentist and fewer holidays than he would have wished. In contrast to his wife, in his non-work time he mixed more widely and participated in many more leisure activities. Mr Kelly was also an active member of his profession and regularly went on courses and to conferences, sometimes abroad; whereas Mrs Kelly's equally considerable involvement in her domestic work led only to greater isolation.

The tendency for married women to return to paid work is more common during this third stage and among the research couples who conformed to this pattern the marital struggle for leisure was a conspicuous feature of family life. In research family no. 21, both the husband and the wife worked full-time outside the home, but only the wife worked full-time inside the home. This was most marked at weekends when the husband played golf on both Saturdays and Sundays, but Mrs Jarvis only did so on Sundays. On Saturdays she caught up on 'her' housework. According to the questionnaire data, the wife in this dual career family did all the cooking, cleaning, washing, ironing and tidying-up (with assistance from a paid domestic worker) and most of the shopping. She was remarkably uncomplaining about this workload, except to note how tiring it all was. The sense of pride in being able to cope with two jobs and the sense of service to others, particularly her husband, pervaded the separate interview with Mrs Jarvis: '[The role of a wife] First of all to be there to look after the man, I think that men do basically need this. I think to keep law and order in the house so that the man can live a comfortable existence because I think that men do like comfort and it is part of a good wife's job to run the home in this way.'

In another late dual-career family, the working wife's burden was partially alleviated by the presence of ageing kin nearby. In research family no. 27, Mr and Mrs Green both worked outside the home, both disliked domestic work, and both were highly enthusiastic about their many leisure pursuits. However, although the grandparents helped with the children and did the shopping, Mrs Green did the bulk of the housework and took the major responsibility for the children. Consequently, while Mr Green stayed late to work at the university, his wife collected the children and prepared the dinner. Mr Green spent his vacations on political activities while Mrs Green took the children on holiday.

Thus not all late career couples, and especially late career wives, were able to spend an increasing amount of time on leisure activities unrelated to their major role responsibilities. Although the amount of leisure time available to professional workers and their wives tended to increase throughout the family and work cycles, the trend was subject to a number of modifications and as a result was experienced very unevenly in practice.

In addition to the case-study data used in the above analysis of leisure, supporting evidence of a more representative kind can be found in a variety of sources. A National Survey of Leisure concluded that the availability of leisure time and the selection of leisure pursuits indeed varied over the life-cycle (Sillitoe, 1969). More specifically, the survey noted that among married women with children many of their leisure pursuits 'were indistinguishable from normal household duties' (ibid., p. 45). Wives aged between 23 and 45 also mentioned 'family or domestic reasons' far more frequently than husbands 'for taking part in sports and games less often now than in the past' (ibid., pp. 132-3). In the present study, although the husbands also engaged in many domestic-work-related leisure activities (for example, building and repairing shelves) and work-career-related leisure activities (for example, reading journals), they reported many more 'pure' leisure interests than the wives. The problem of different levels of male and female participation in sport and informal recreation was highlighted by Hillman and Whalley (1977). They found that the greater leisure activity rate of men compared to women was associated with access to the use of a car and that generally women were at a disadvantage in this respect.

The time dimension of leisure has been thoroughly researched in a cross-cultural survey of twelve societies (Szalai, 1972). Among other things this project emphasised 'that the problems faced by the working woman have not been adequately solved in any of the countries surveyed, and substantial inequities in the division of labour by sex remain everywhere' (ibid., p. 121). For example, employed men reported more free time on days off than either employed women or housewives, and more free time on workdays than employed women. Only in the case of a comparison between employed men and house-wives did men report slightly less free time on workdays (ibid., p. 131).

The time budgets of married couples have also been studied by Meissner in Canada who found (1977, p. 167):

> The day of married women adapts extensively to the requirements of younger children and a paying job, while the day of men, parti-cularly their workday, remains essentially the same. The force which shapes women's day is work, and their available free time suffers under the pressure of more work. Even on weekends, women's spare time is reduced step by step as demands are greater, while men have more leisure hours even under the most demanding conditions than women in the easiest circumstances.

The extent of leisure inequalities within marriage among all socio-economic groups is documented by Young and Willmott in their study of the symmetrical family. In their chapter on leisure there are ten 'men only' tables, four tables that include men and women, and no tables for women only. In the 'mixed' tables, Young and Willmott show that men watch more television than women (1973, p. 213), men have more leisure activities than women (ibid., p. 219), and that men see more friends and relatives than women (ibid., p. 229). Young and Willmott also comment that wives mostly 'knitted or sewed more than they did anything else except watch television' (ibid., p. 217). Thus, the leisure time and activities of husbands and wives cannot be understood in isolation from an unequal sexual division of labour that allocates the main responsibility for the home to women and the main responsibility for 'breadwinning' to men.

Leisure and power

In an important sense much of what has been discussed so far in this chapter is indicative of the husband's power legitimately to avoid certain activities and engage in others. Consequently, when greater opportunities for leisure occur, married women are not always able to take advantage of them. The separation of home from work and the fact that housework is primarily unpaid and unskilled, and therefore widely regarded as an unimportant activity, seems to facilitate the tendency for more free time to mean more leisure for men but not necessarily for women.

Conventional stereotypes of appropriate masculine and feminine behaviour further restrict the leisure options of both men and women. For example, among the research families I found no evidence of the wives being interested in or participating in carpentry and car maintenance and not one wife reported going to a pub or club alone. Similarly, I found no evidence among the husbands in the sample of an interest in flower-arranging, knitting or sewing. The tendency for different interests and activities to have specific gender associations clearly discourages the vast majority of men and women from participating in a range of pursuits that they might otherwise enjoy. In the absence of any evidence to the contrary, one can confidently suggest that such patterns are learnt, probably from a very early age (Dahlstrom, 1967).[5]

In addition to sex-linked role responsibilities and expectations that constrain in various ways a spouse's choice of leisure pursuits, there is the problem of which member of the marital dyad, if any, has most influence on a couple's leisure patterns. Among the research families, data on this aspect of leisure were collected at several points during the interviews with the husbands and wives together and separately, and some of this material has been alluded to in other contexts. In a less *ad hoc* manner it can be shown that it is usually the husband who is most dominant in this as in other 'important' areas of family life.

The collection of social network data revealed that in nineteen of the research families (or 50 per cent) the husband was the major source of friends although most of the friends were subsequently regarded as 'joint' by the couples. Phrases such as 'I found them and she became friends with the wives' (research family no. 35), and 'originally these friends were all mine, now they are joint' (research family no. 37) were commonly used to describe this pattern. In the other nineteen families, eighteen claimed that the husband and wife initiated friendships with equal frequency, and in one case the couple reported that they had virtually no friends (research family no. 33). Upon further investigation, in the second group of couples, in which neither partner was the dominant friend-maker, most of the close friends tended originally to be the husband's, whereas the wife tended to be the main source of casual friendships. For example, in research family no. 18, the husband's 'old rock-climbing friend' had become the couple's most intimate friend. The husbands had introduced their respective wives to each other and now the two families went on holiday together. In contrast, the neighbourhood was frequently mentioned by the wives as a source of friends but such relationships rarely survived geographical mobility. These findings suggest that husband dominance in this area is in fact greater than the basic figures on friendship relationships imply. These findings are also comparable to those of Babchuk and Bates who, in a study entitled 'The primary relations of middle-class couples' in America, concluded that 'couples give the appearance of being egalitarian, but in the sphere of friendships the male predominates' (1963, p. 384).

In the case of various leisure decisions concerned with holidays, weekends, staying in or going out, and so on, it will be recalled that in research family no. 1 the wife expressed a preference for holidays alone with her husband and child, but always conceded and went to her husband's parents. Additional data that confirm the impression that it is the husband who tends to have most say in these matters are presented below.

> Mr Bates regarded holidays as crucial. Mrs Bates said that 'sometimes I would like to stay and spend holiday money on the house, but we always go'.　　　　　　　　　　　(Research Family No. 9)

> Mrs Sims was a full-time housewife who enjoyed going out during the evenings, but Mr Sims did not. The leisure pattern in this family was rarely to go out: 'I would like to go out for meals but we don't . . . my husband is one for coming home and staying here and I'm one for going out.'　　　　　(Research Family No. 4)

Mr and Mrs Fox regularly visited the husband's parents. Mrs Fox commented that she disliked this 'routine', but that her husband did not, and every Sunday they visited Mr Fox's parents.

(Research Family No. 16)

Mrs Frazer said that she enjoyed the theatre and opera, but that they never went to either because her husband did not want to.

(Research Family No. 17)

Mrs Read listed a number of things that she would like to change, including going out for more meals, better holidays, and 'more time with my husband at weekends—they are too short and involved'. Mr Read's comments on these possible changes to their style of life were that home cooking was just as good; they could not afford 'better holidays'; and he enjoyed playing and watching sports at weekends. (Research Family No. 11)

The issue of the husband's sporting proclivities was raised in many families. For example, Mr Fox (research family no. 16) insisted on playing and watching sport at every opportunity and commented: 'I like sport and she doesn't and can't understand my attitude to it.' Mrs Jarvis (research family no. 21) said that she 'took up golf in self-defence' and claimed that she now enjoyed it. The extent of husband domination in the area of leisure can be judged from the fact that only one couple reported husband disapproval of the wife's extensive leisure activities. Mrs Wade (research family no. 38) was extremely active in local politics and had recently been ill. Mr Wade made the following comment:

It does tend to throw an extra burden on myself and having admitted to being domestically capable I find myself doing domestic chores which I have come to accept. I would much rather not but it is a question of necessity.

Thus the combination of public service and ill-health had enabled the wife in this family to absent herself legitimately from certain household tasks and to take advantage of the opportunities for increased leisure that an affluent mid-career situation provided. Apart from this atypical case, the trend was for the husband to dominate most leisure decisions that affected the family.

Finally, the tendency for husbands to be able to list a greater number of leisure activities that were unconnected with work or domestic work, compared to their wives at all stages of the family cycle, suggests that husbands are somewhat less constrained in their leisure choices. Consequently, husbands not only had more influence on the family situation, they also had more control over their own lives, in contrast to the majority of wives who seemed far more immersed in their primary role of housewife.

Most of my interests have gone; too involved in the family.
(Wife, Research Family No. 8)

All my interests involve the necessities of life like housework and college preparation. If I had more time I would clean the house more.   (Wife, Research Family No. 12)

No time for anything else except family and home, especially children.   (Wife, Research Family No. 2)

Some wives equated their lack of leisure interests with being an uninteresting person; among such wives a typical sentiment was 'I sound awfully dull, don't I?' (research family no. 36). Another wife tried to discourage any further questions on this topic by saying 'I have three small children, you know, which takes a lot of time' (research family no. 16).

In this chapter it has been suggested that for the most part women are invisible in studies of leisure.[6] Ironically, the amount of weekday leisure time available to many of the mid- and late career full-time housewives in this study was often considerable. However, in most other respects it was the husband who tended to have more leisure time, report a greater number of leisure interests and activities and generally dominate certain leisure choices. The reasons for this pattern of leisure inequalities within marriage can nearly all be traced to the basic sexual division of labour in which men are primarily responsible for paid work and women for domestic work.

Notes: Chapter 6

1 For a review of the literature, see Parker (1972 and 1976), particularly his references to the work of Kaplan, DeGrazia, Anderson and Smigel.
2 See Parker (1976), who briefly discusses 'Leisure and social stratification in Britain' and includes a few other references to inequality and leisure in a basic text that purports to cover 'the whole field of leisure'.
3 See Roberts, 1970.
4 Group one consisted of families in which the husband was under 35 years old and the majority of the children were aged 5 or under. Group two were families in which the husband was aged between 36 and 40 years and the majority of the children were aged between 6 and 11 years. In group three families the husband was 41 years of age or above and the majority of the children were 12 years of age or older. There were nine couples who could not be neatly allocated to one of these groups on

the basis of these operational definitions; therefore they were categorised by reference to the husband's work career stage by occupational grade.

5   A visit to a park and a count of the number of unescorted school-age boys and girls will reveal the extent to which public places and certain activities are male-dominated from an early age.

6   An excellent example of the problem of female invisibility, apart from those already noted, concerns the survey by Roberts, Cook, Clark and Semeonoff (1976). The title of the article is 'The family cycle, domestic roles and the meaning of leisure', but the study was based solely on a sample of '474 economically active males'. If the sample had consisted of females only, the title of the work would no doubt have reflected this fact.

CHAPTER 7

The Work and Domestic Work Experiences of Husbands and Wives

The significance and implications of the prevailing sexual division of labour in which husbands are primarily responsible for economic provision and wives for housework and child-care has underpinned the whole of this study. Here, this division of labour based on sex will be examined as an ongoing experience in the lives of professional workers and their wives at the child-rearing stage of the family cycle.

Among the thirty-eight professionally employed husbands who were studied, the whole range of known professional work experiences and attitudes was represented (Elliott, 1972). In other words, all the husbands conformed in varying degrees to the following model of a professional work career:

1 Lengthy and specialised occupational training and socialisation.
2 Formal occupational qualification and membership of a professional association.
3 High occupational interest, autonomy and commitment.
4 Relatively privileged work, market and status situation.

The notion that 'the critical anchorage of the characteristic male role is to his occupation or career' (Turner, 1970, p. 255) was amply confirmed by the professional husbands in this study. In response to a hypothetical question concerning winning or inheriting a sum of money sufficient to live without working, the vast majority of husbands (thirty-six out of a total of thirty-eight) were quite emphatic that they would not retire. Work was too interesting, enjoyable, gratifying and generally too central in their lives. Some husbands even expressed surprise at the question and many thought that a large sum of money would not alter their lives markedly.

Wouldn't retire, makes you feel you are doing something positive, keeping things moving.   (Industrial Scientist)

I like the work, wouldn't be happy all day at home.

(Industrial Scientist)

Would not retire, would not make much difference. (Academic)

I think an academic job is a fantastic job for a gentleman. Tremendous freedom; wouldn't retire; need something to keep your mind occupied, obviously. (Academic)

Not bothered. In fact anyone who has a good income has enough money. Would give extra to charity, put some by for kids.

(Academic)

Oh no. I wouldn't retire, I enjoy my work. (Academic)

I wouldn't retire because I am very fulfilled by work. I enjoy it. It appeals to several different facets of my character so that if I had a lot of money I wouldn't cease to work. (Dentist)

The reasons given for not wanting to retire and the separate discussions with each husband about his work career (see below) overwhelmingly suggested that the husbands were positively attached to their work, and that it had great personal significance for them. Some husbands were actively looking for ways to increase their sense of achievement and involvement in work, such as six husbands who did not want to retire but would take the opportunity to 'experiment' and change careers. All six were industrial scientists and five of them were between the ages of 41 and 50. Three aspired to become self-employed and the others were thinking in terms of careers characterised by what they regarded as greater social value, for example, teaching and social work. Thus, the possibility of a life of leisure was rejected by every husband except two, and one of those expected to 'be bored within a year' (research family no. 23). The most frequently mentioned items of potential expenditure were investments, houses, holidays and cars. Mr Thompson (research family no. 36) neatly summarised many of the responses when he noted: 'Wouldn't retire. I enjoy my work, probably work less, take more holidays, move to bigger house, bigger car, but wouldn't drastically change our life pattern.'

In marked contrast to the professionally employed husbands, the 'critical anchorage' of the female role involved reference to both the home and motherhood. Among the thirty-six wives who were interviewed, all had primary responsibility for the care of the home and the children. Attachment to motherhood was both considerable and positive, whereas attachment to the housework dimension was predictably far more ambiguous, comprising a mixture of positive and negative values well known to researchers in this area (Gavron, 1966; Lopata, 1972; Oakley, 1974). Motherhood was experienced as a highly rewarding activity, but housework tended to be experienced very much in the way it is described by Oakley on the basis of her study of twenty middle-class and twenty working-class housewives, namely:

1 As a monotonous, fragmented and relentless job.
2 Associated with feelings of inadequacy, housebound loneliness and general dissatisfaction.
3 Highly valued for the autonomy and variety of the role.
4 As a role conferring relatively low status and involving considerable economic dependence.

Data that illustrate many of these familiar features of the housewife role have been quoted already, especially in the previous two chapters. What follows therefore is a supplementary selection biased towards the motherhood aspect.

Nice to be at home with the children . . . Cleaning bores me to tears but has to be done. What I like about being at home is organising my own time as far as possible and doing things I like doing, for example, decorating and cooking. I do miss meeting people though.
(Industrial Scientist's Wife)

Happy at home. I like all the things connected with being at home apart from cleaning. You get a certain amount of freedom from being alone.　　　　　　　　　　　　(Industrial Scientist's Wife)

I find housework extremely boring, which can't possibly occupy all my time. Just don't want to waste the next thirty years of my life.　　　　　　　　　　　　　　　　(Industrial Scientist's Wife)

[Career?] Oh, no, no, no. I don't regret it at all, much rather have the children now than a career. I wouldn't swop them for a career, put it that way . . . I don't really enjoy being on my own at home, get a bit miserable. Have plenty to do all day but get a bit fed up and irritated sometimes. Housework a repetitive process that never seems to get you anywhere. People come and mess it all up and you have to start all over again.　　　　　　(Industrial Scientist's Wife)

I enjoy having babies and looking after them . . . enjoyed full-time work but enjoy being at home more though I sometimes get fed up. Going out to work wouldn't improve that, only make it worse.

I do all the housework. I expected James to help when the children were little, like bath them.   (Academic's Wife)

I enjoy looking after the children and I enjoy being a housewife and I'm not particularly bothered about them going to school. I like them. I like them as people really ... I think my children need me. I remember when I was young; getting home and my mother being there, even when I was working. You know, she was the home in a sense; and I think the children think like this—they think of mum and the home together.   (Academic's Wife)

[Full-time work?] No, not while the children were young. [Housework?] Anyone can do it as far as I am concerned.   (Dentist's Wife)

A preference for child-care activities rather than domestic tasks was expressed by virtually every couple. Whilst the husbands tended to 'give' a token amount of help on a discretionary basis, the impact of their 'help' was felt mainly in the area of child-care activities.[1] The wives were prepared to pay for domestic help but were not at all keen for others to care for their children.

Not prepared to reverse roles permanently. But for a short period, yes, for children's sake. Couldn't do as good job as my wife [in child-care], and I couldn't get any long-term satisfaction from housekeeping.   (Industrial Scientist)

[Role reversal?] [Long pause] Perhaps not to the extent that I do. I can think of more interesting things than washing dishes. My own view is that mothers should not go out to work until children are at school; need close contact in the early years. Whether they do it better or not I don't know. I wouldn't do it as a full-time job.
                              (Dentist)

I wouldn't go out to work if it meant that I had got to find someone else to look after them. I've got to see them off in the morning and be here when they come home in the evening.   (Dentist's Wife)

If you have a choice and have children, should remain at home with them for the first part of their lives. Especially if you have made the decision to have children you are missing out on seeing them develop, that is very interesting.   (Academic's Wife)

I think that children need their mother at home when they come home from school. I don't think it is right for them to let themselves in with a key. Obviously when something happens at school they want to tell you then, not an hour later when you come home. I think this is essential. [Domestic help?] Yes, when the children were young, not now.   (Industrial Scientist's Wife)

All the wives studied except one (who had left university to get married) had worked until marriage, predominantly and typically in 'service' occupations.[2] Out of the thirty-six wives interviewed, twenty-four continued to work after marriage up until the birth of their first child and six of these had since returned to paid work (four part-time and two full-time), two wives had continued in paid work apart from a short period of maternity leave (one part-time and one full-time), and only ten wives had ceased paid work completely upon marriage. Among the latter group, the main reason given for leaving work was that marriage coincided with the husband changing the location of his work, and in one case the wife said that her 'husband thought it was appropriate' (research family no. 4). Thus, irrespective of whether or not the wife worked outside the home after marriage, it was assumed that the wife undertook primary responsibility for the home and subsequently the children. Although the husband in every instance correspondingly assumed the role of breadwinner in a similarly ascriptive manner, his actual occupation was an achieved role *par excellence* and contained markedly fewer sources of discontent. Presenting the two sex-based work roles in this way therefore reveals a number of interesting and instructive points for comparison.

The separate interviews with each husband indicated that they all experienced considerable satisfaction with their work careers and general life situation. In the main they found their work roles extrinsically and intrinsically rewarding, spoke highly of their respective professions and had few if any regrets about their chosen occupations. When asked about the aspects of their work they most 'liked' they all emphasised the following dimensions: 'control', 'variety', 'challenge', 'interest', 'freedom', 'autonomy' and 'social contact'. Among the most frequently mentioned 'disliked' aspects were 'paperwork', 'meetings', 'routine activities' and occasionally the behaviour of subordinates and superiors; in a phrase, bureaucratic administration. Significantly, the responses elicited by open-ended questions produced a qualitatively and quantitatively greater list of 'likes' than 'dislikes'. In fact, some of the husbands were hard-pressed to think of any 'dislikes' and commented to this effect: 'dislike is too strong a term' (industrial scientist, research family no. 22), and one respondent simply replied 'nothing' (academic, research family no. 25).

The dentists were distinctive in two respects: they, more frequently than others, commented on the 'creative' and 'service' aspects of their work; and without exception registered their aversion to the physical and mental demands of dentistry (Eccles and Powell, 1967; Slack and Page, 1969). Thus, notwithstanding the positive attractions and benefits of dentistry, the arduous nature of the work was vividly expressed by three of the dentists included in the study.

It is very hard work. I come home extremely tired because for a start you are disliked. People are afraid of you and you have got to persuade them to sit there while you hurt them. One tries to keep the pain to a minimum even if it is only the prick of a needle and then it goes numb. None the less you are giving them something unpleasant and he dislikes you for it. And you have got to win him over to have the treatment, to come back again and like you, and this takes a tremendous mental and emotional strain.

The strain each day is enormous. It really is very exhausting work, to keep one's patience and to keep a smile. It is very hard work and long hours to earn the money.

In dentistry you are often working on frightened people. Let me put it this way. I am doing a fairly intricate job. But can you imagine any job where you are working on an endless belt principle for such long hours, with such a critical audience? Every day, every move you make is being watched and you are aware of it. No leeway to make any mistakes, and in addition to that your patient is very apprehensive. A friend of mine told me that every time he had an attack of angina in the surgery he was working late to catch up. If you have a difficult patient for fifteen minutes, I have to sit down afterwards. Two highly apprehensive children for ten minutes each and you can feel busted for the rest of the morning. A tense patient just drains the energy out of a dentist.

In general, however, the professional workers studied, including the dentists, were essentially well satisfied with their chosen careers. Disappointments, if any, were on the whole limited to minor and/or single aspects of their work, and certainly had not induced the vast majority of them to regret entering their particular field of professional specialisation. For example, the career disappointments of the bureaucratically employed professional workers ranged from problems and prospects connected with salaries and promotion to concern with too little or excessive geographical mobility. Three industrial scientists felt mildly trapped by the company pension scheme, which in other respects they regarded as excellent. As already indicated, some of the husbands had from time to time considered and rejected various alternative careers. This was not so much because they were disillusioned with their current careers, but wished to seek even greater work satisfaction. For example, Mr Walker (research family no. 15), although he derived 'intellectual satisfaction' from his work as an industrial scientist and had 'no great dislikes', also said that if he was starting out again, he would really 'prefer to teach'. Thus, the high levels of occupational involvement, interest, satisfaction and contentment (and so on) expressed by the husbands are reasonably typical of professional male workers (see, for example, Caplow, 1964; Vollmer and Mills, 1966; Hirsch, 1968; Cotgrove and Box, 1970).

In contrast to their husbands, the wives were far from satisfied and content with their work role(s) and life situation. In a majority of cases a deep sense of dissatisfaction pervaded the separate interviews with the wives. Among the full-time housewives studied, the major source of discontent seemed to revolve around the lack of a sense of achievement beyond the private world of the family.

Mrs Harrop, the wife of an industrial scientist, felt that leaving work to become a full-time mother and housewife had a detrimental effect on her work career as a lecturer in further education and stressed that 'This part of my life has suffered'.

Mrs Sims, the wife of an industrial scientist, regretted not working since marriage and would have done 'if conditions were better, such as a car and training and I could get a job to fit into school holidays'. Mrs Sims also faced the problem of her husband's approval: 'Husband doesn't want me to work.'

Mrs Moss, the wife of an industrial scientist, commented: 'I do not regret giving up full-time work but wished I had done more in life than just bring up children. Remembered for more, something really worthwhile.'

Mrs Ash, the wife of an industrial scientist, said that she had no intention of ever returning to work although she had 'always wanted to be a nurse'.

Mrs Bates, the wife of an industrial scientist, commented that she did not want to move to the north, but did, and consequently misses her family. Her main interests included 'many little things like sewing, knitting and baking. Do not have much time, read very little, a few magazines and newspapers.' Mrs Bates was a nurse before marriage and hoped to return on a part-time basis when her children were older. In the meantime she noted: 'I miss the work; meeting people; my own money.'

Mrs Walker, the wife of an industrial scientist, said that she would like to go back to work but that it 'depends on what arrangements I can make for children returning from school. Like to train as a teacher, holidays fit in well and a job which fits in very well with running a family. To develop myself as a person; earning my own money; able to stand on my own two feet if it was necessary.'

Mrs Frazer, the wife of an industrial scientist, was currently trying to gain enough qualifications to enable her to train as a teacher, which she regarded as the 'sort of job that is interesting, useful and has the right sort of hours to combine with family life . . . I think unless I can do something in the next couple of years I have wasted what intelligence I have. I'm not stupid. Wouldn't work unless I had somebody to come in and do the chores.'

Mrs Price, the wife of an industrial scientist, said that although she thought that mothers should be at home when the children were young, she had 'always fancied teaching'. But her husband 'didn't want me to go out to work, old-fashioned in this way'. Mrs Price was now aged 47 and 'very much' regretted not having a career. 'Especially this past ten years, I feel that I wasted a lot of opportunities . . . if I had my time over again I certainly would have taken a career. But I still wouldn't have done it while the children were young.' On her role as a full-time housewife Mrs Price commented: 'I am not in the habit of thinking deeply. Housewife doesn't need to think. Don't have to think to clean, cook or wash. These come naturally to you.'

Mrs Kay, the wife of an industrial scientist, commented that she was 'not qualified for anything, not qualified to do anything interesting and rewarding. And I don't want to go back to work unless it was interesting . . . [Do you regret not having a career?] In some ways, for my own personal satisfaction. But in lots of ways it makes for better harmony in the home if I'm not yearning to go back to work. Not a frustrated career woman tied to the sink. In isolation, I would have liked the satisfaction of a career, but in the context of marriage, no. It's been quite a good thing that I've not had one.'

Mrs Lyon, an academic's wife, was a teacher before she had children and, like most of the wives, disapproved of mothers with young children working outside the home. She described her full-time housewife role in the following terms: 'I get very frustrated that I have got to do the routine jobs; dishes, kids, shopping, etc . . . it is quite tedious having two babies screaming all day.' On her teaching career, she noted: 'Like to stretch my mind, don't like junior work, like to keep up to date. I like the power; the children; the companionship of colleagues.' Mrs Lyon felt that she was now 'getting rusty', but indicated that she looked forward to returning to work, perhaps 'do research for a change, stretch my mind'.

The above extracts, plus the data already presented, suggest that the professional worker's wife who does not work outside the home tends to experience the housewife role as one that consists of a number of interrelated dissatisfying elements. First, domestic work was not regarded as a source of lasting intrinsic or extrinsic satisfaction and, consequently, was not highly valued by the housewives in this study: quite the reverse—considerable personal devaluation seemed to be associated with the housework role. As one full-time housewife so cogently put it: 'plenty to do but nothing to think about' (research family no. 24). In the light of the known similarity between housework as work and repetitive and relatively unskilled factory work (Oakley, 1974, p. 182), the fundamentally dissatisfying character of housework reported in this study was to be expected.

However, the analogy is not entirely accurate. At the very least, unlike factory workers, the full-time housewife is more or less economically dependent upon her husband.[3] The significance of this economic subjection can and does permeate the whole conjugal role relationship and in particular the distribution of power and scarce resources between husbands and wives. Some of the main consequences of the widespread tendency to allocate primary responsibility for the home and children to women have been well summarised by Holter (1970, p. 46):

> First, the specialisation places limits on her training for other activities. Whereas men gain competence in an internal family role as well as an external role, women's skills are mainly relevant only to the family. This places men naturally as co-ordinators of external and internal tasks, they know both the family and the external world. Moreover, men's external roles give them direct access to the material resources of society, and this is the basis for a power position. Women's access to such resources is typically indirect, that is, through their husbands.

The characteristic economic and social dependence of so many adults is an increasing anomaly in a society that places a premium on economic self-reliance. From the standpoint of the individual housewife, such a situation is unlikely to alleviate the sense of personal inadequacy reported by many of the wives. In the absence of the conditions that are conducive to a collective response to what may be regarded as an economically and socially deprived situation, resistance can take individual forms that are often highly detrimental to the health and well-being of women. Rowbotham (1973) lists many of the psychological and physical symptoms including hysteria, nervous complaints, agoraphobia, headaches and depression. A recent and thoroughgoing study of depression in women amply confirms the relationship between social situation and certain types of illness (Brown and Harris, 1978).

In the present study, for nearly every full-time housewife a feeling of a lack of fulfilment also contributed to a high level of dissatisfaction. This feeling was not unrelated to the view that housework was thought to be intellectually limited, uninteresting, isolating and generally unworthy. It may well be that the widely indicated sensitivity to their lack of achievement and contribution outside the home and family was heightened by an invidious occupational comparison between themselves, their husbands and selected members of their social network. At the same time, the frequent laughter by the wives during certain sections of their interview schedule suggests that many of them found questions about paid work and domestic work quite embarrassing (Hobson, 1978, pp. 81-2). Thus, a pattern of repressing one's own interests, individuality and long-held occupational career aspirations was discernible and could be considered one more element in the full-time housewife's essentially subordinate and unenviable predicament.

The few sources of positive evaluation available to the housewife were themselves subject to distinct limitations. For example, autonomy was severely circumscribed in a variety of ways that have already been alluded to in the earlier chapters. Similarly, the mother role is inherently short-term. The tendency for husbands to participate more often in child-care tasks than certain repetitive and time-consuming domestic tasks can lead to a further extension of the husband's area of competence and power and a corresponding erosion of the wife's.[4]

Such is the fate of most full-time housewives in this and other studies (Lopata, 1972; Oakley, 1974). One of the increasingly favoured alternatives is for the wife to seek employment (Central Statistical Office, 1974). This strategy, however, is fraught with difficulties for the wife. There is abundant evidence to show that women who enter the labour market are treated differently from men (Hunt, 1968; Mackie and Pattullo, 1977). Briefly, compared to men, women tend to receive lower pay, are restricted to a narrower range of occupations and experience slimmer chances for promotion. These, and other occupational comparisons that reflect adversely on women, have led Barron and Norris (1976) to speak of the existence of a 'dual labour market'.

However, prior to entry to the world of work, women typically have to overcome certain socialisation practices and beliefs which maintain that paid work is more important for men than women.[5] Also, many married women in this and other studies have to seek their husband's approval before going out to work. Finally, a married woman who wishes to take this step is often constrained to select an occupation that is compatible with her domestic role. In other words, she must choose a job that interferes as little as possible with her ability to attend

Middle-Class Couples

to the bulk of the housework and the rest of the family's needs; a job that is conducive to her remaining available to 'serve' others.

> If I wanted to go back to work and it was convenient for me and for other members of the family, then I think he would be happy. I don't think he would like me to find a job where the children would have to let themselves in when they came home from school. If it 'cocked-up' the family like that, then I don't think he would be very pleased at all.   (Full-Time Housewife)

> As long as he gets his creature comforts he is OK. Difficult to run a home and work full-time.   (Part-Time Teacher and Housewife)

> He didn't mind me doing that part-time job; didn't conflict with the children. But he would not be very keen if the children had to be pushed around; we couldn't manage the entertaining; or I wasn't there to provide the meals and things. I think this would affect the relationship at home.   (Full-Time Housewife)

> I would like to go back to work but husband wouldn't like me to put baby in a nursery, thinks I ought to be at home. Eventually like to return to work part-time; he wouldn't mind part-time. He was always able to come home and his mother was there and he wants his children to be the same.   (Full-Time Housewife)

Phrases such as 'able to fit in with the family', 'adequate arrangements', 'so long as the home ran smoothly' and 'he likes his meal on the table when he comes in in the evening' were typical of the comments among the housewives who were not active in a full-time work career. The prominence of teaching as the stated and actual career preference among the wives of this study testifies to the rigidity and influence of the prevailing sexual division of labour in relation to the occupational choices of women married to professional workers. [6]
This division of labour is further reflected in the incidence of and reasons given for part-time work by married women (Young and Willmott, 1973; pp. 104-9; Mackie and Pattullo, 1977, pp. 41-3). Moreover, the possible disadvantages of part-time work in terms of satisfaction from family, leisure and especially work activities and interests suggest that such a strategy is in many respects a false panacea. Part-time work for married women is notoriously poorly paid, and typically involves very restricted occupational choices and limited chances for training and promotion. All these drawbacks are in excess of those normally experienced by women workers (Counter Information Services, 1976; Mackie and Pattullo, 1977).

Irrespective of the occupational destination of married women, the evidence from this and many other studies strongly suggests that in dual-job or career families the traditional sexual division of labour in the home is not radically altered and that basic role responsibilities persist (Rapoport and Rapoport, 1971; Szalai, 1972; Young and Willmott, 1973). In the present study, when Mrs Green (research family no. 27), a full-time teacher, wanted to attend a conference or course, she had first of all to make arrangements for her three children. When Mr Green went away he was faced with no such problem. Similarly, it has already been noted how in another dual-career family (research family no. 19), the husband only marginally and selectively increased his level of participation in domestic and child-care tasks. In these circumstances the 'working mother' is likely to experience considerable work pressure, fatigue and loss of leisure time. For example, Mrs Jarvis (research family no. 21), a full-time teacher, described her situation in the following terms:

I try not to let the work impinge on the family . . . There are times when I do feel tired and I think it would be nice to have a rest . . . To be honest, especially at the end of term there are times when I am more tired than I would normally be . . . I try to give them as much home cooking as I can and I try and organise it. But I probably don't spend quite as much time . . . on bottling jam that I would normally do. It all has to be rather more streamlined.

Part-time career women also reported that they 'suffered' from fatigue and a lack of time. For instance, Mrs Jackson (research family no. 3) worked as a teacher two days a week and sometimes more if requested and commented: 'I enjoy schoolwork more than housework.' Mrs Jackson employed domestic help, yet in general she said that she had 'less time to take an interest in and talk to' her family and less time 'to enjoy life' with her husband.

Another dual-career family problem that tends to involve the wife in a greater degree of adaptation and inconvenience compared to the husband concerns the possibility of conflict between the demands of the couple's respective work careers. In this study, for example, Mrs Harding (research family no. 19), whose salary exceeded that of her husband, reported an 'occasion once when we both had a course booked for the same week. He went. We decided that his career was more important than mine.' In a study of dual-career families in America, comparable career dilemmas were 'resolved more in favour of the husband' (Holmstrom, 1972, p. 156), and another study found that 'the husband's migration influences not only the career development of the wife, but also the initial choice of career' (Long, 1974,

p. 348). It seems, therefore, that in the case of dual-career families, the husband's career is often advanced at the expense of the wife's. I have found no evidence for the reverse.

To summarise, among the research families, the pattern was for the wives to subordinate their interests, both work and non-work, in various ways to the interests of their husbands. Briefly, if the wife remained at home her role as mother might often be experienced as satisfying. However, she typically experienced a great sense of unfulfilment and even uselessness in other respects. If she undertook paid work in addition to her domestic responsibilities, her work career achievements and rewards were usually lower than her husband's and she still had the house and the children to care for, or at the least organise.[7]

With reference to the earlier discussion of different forms of marital equality, although it could be argued that the relative contributions of the spouses are different but comparable in certain respects, it could also be argued that the highly gender-based nature of the division of labour seems on balance to confer mostly advantages on husbands and mostly disadvantages on wives. Generally the traditional female contribution is evaluated differently from that of the males; the housewife's work is unpaid, unskilled, uninteresting and unpraised; the husband's work in this study was highly paid, skilled, interesting and well regarded. Moreover, whilst the breadwinning role is a source of great power and legitimate authority, the homemaking role tends to involve dependence and subordination. Thus, it is not so much the content of work and domestic work roles that is important, but the socioeconomic context and its implications. To quote Braverman: 'what is important is not the determinate form of labour but its *social form*' (1974, p. 362). The value of domestic labour in the home, and therefore the housewife's value, is obscured primarily by its unpaid character in a type of society that in other respects is dominated by money and the market (Marx, 1970; Weber, 1976).[8]

Notes: Chapter 7

1 See the data presented earlier in this study and by Oakley (1974, p. 138). Of particular significance is the tendency for husbands to 'help' in the home in a highly selective manner, mainly in the non-routine and more creative activities, including 'do-it-yourself' housework.

2 Among the thirty-eight families included in this study, twenty-eight of the wives were employed in occupations with a high service content before marriage (ten teachers, eight secretarial workers, four nurses and one each of the following: social worker, cardiographer, physiotherapist, air hostess, canteen manageress and hairdresser). The remaining ten wives were employed as follows: six laboratory workers, two computer programmers, one scientist and one student.

3 For an analysis of the relationship between wage labour and domestic labour, see

Secombe (1973 and 1975), Gardiner (1975) and Coulson, Magas and Wainwright (1975).

4 Goode (1970, p. 70) and Harris (1977, p. 81) have made the same point with regard to domestic activities.

5 Women also have to contend with the exhortations of elected and self-appointed moral entrepreneurs, the conservative media, including the advertising industry, all of whom tend to glorify the role of motherhood and by implication deprecate the notion of the 'working mother'. In this context, see the study of women's magazines by White (1970).

6 In this small-scale study, ten wives were already qualified teachers and at least six others were in the process of seriously considering this career, mainly on 'family' grounds. Despite the pervasiveness of the sex-based division of labour in contemporary society, its influence on the occupational aspirations of young girls does not seem to have been fully appreciated by occupational choice theorists (for example, Ford and Box, 1967; Musgrave, 1967). Evidence that corroborates this general point is provided by Timperley and Gregory, who in a study of sixth formers found marked differences in the career choices of males and females. For instance, over two-thirds of the females expressed a wish to enter 'education' compared to under one-third of the males, whereas twice as many males as females expressed a wish to enter 'industry and commerce' (1971, p. 101). No comment or discussion accompanied these dramatic figures in terms of their implications for theories of occupational choice.

7 This is not to deny that professional work involves 'stresses' and 'strains' (see, for example, Cotgrove and Box, 1970), merely to record that they were not emphasised by the respondents in this study.

8 For an excellent summary of some of the arguments and consequences that relate to this point, see Rowbotham (1973).

CHAPTER 8

Concluding Discussion

Summary of the main findings

During the course of this study the view that conjugal role relationships in industrial capitalist societies are in the process of becoming less segregated and more egalitarian has been subjected to a critical review. More specifically, with the aid of a sample of professional workers and their wives at the child-rearing stage of the family life-cycle, severe doubts have been raised with respect to the 'middle-class' variant of this thesis.

In a more positive vein, the material presented in this study exemplifies and supports the alternative claim that marital relationships remain highly segregated, unequal and husband-dominated. Among the professional workers and their wives investigated, a majority reported that the wife typically performed a distinct range of domestic and child-rearing tasks considerably more often than the husband, and generally deferred to the husband's authority in the 'more important' areas of decision-making. The least segregated area of the household division of labour was child-care behaviour, though in families with pre-school children in which the wife was a full-time housewife, the wife's domestic workload was particularly onerous. The minor exception of child-care behaviour seemed to be due partly to the availability of the spouses and partly to the husband's willingness to perform child-care more often than other kinds of household tasks. It was also evident from the data that conjugal role behaviour in all areas seemed to vary over the family life-cycle in response to the spouses' changing relationship to the economic division of labour outside the home and constraints emanating from changes in the family situation itself. However, neither the work nor family career cycles were found to be the major influences on the conjugal role patterns described. Instead it was suggested that the husband's orientation to paid work, plus the wife's orientation to domestic work, and to a lesser extent each spouse's orientation to leisure (all of which were susceptible to changes over time as indicated above), seemed to be the main factors that affected the degree of conjugal role segregation. This hypothesis complements and extends the suggestion by Rosser and Harris (1965) to the effect that the greater the woman's interest and involvement in domesticity, the more segregated the conjugal role relationship. Thus, the suggestion by Bott that in loose-knit social networks 'Husbands had to help their wives because their wives got less help from relatives and neighbours' (1971, p. 80) was not found to be the case in the present study.

Fundamental to the operation of these influences was the sexual division of labour whereby the husband takes primary responsibility for paid work and the wife takes primary responsibility for domestic work. This arrangement between the sexes, and the ideas associated with it, seemed to be a basic and pervasive factor upon which 'variations of detail' (Bott, 1971, p. 54) were predicated. The husband, by virtue of his greater participation in the external economic division of labour compared to his wife, was able legitimately to avoid many household tasks and legitimately to dominate family life. To paraphrase Engels (1962, p. 182), the fact that not all husbands use their power does not in the least change the position of the wives. The wife, by virtue of her relative exclusion from paid work and her major responsibility for the home and children, was consigned to economic and social dependence upon her husband. This pattern of responsibilities was entirely congruent with the 'traditional' sex role ideology expressed by the majority of the research couples.

If married women elect to enter the labour market, they often have to gain the approval of their husbands and invariably retain ultimate, though selective, domestic responsibility. As the Rapoports noted in their study of dual-career couples: 'They help with the washing up, they help with changing nappies and so on but there is still a tendency to regard it as *her job* they are helping with' (Rapoport and Rapoport, 1971, p. 304). Upon entry to the labour market, it is apparent that women are more restricted and handicapped than men in a number of respects, notably in connection with occupational choice, income and opportunities for advancement. Unlike men, most married women cannot offer potential employers the same level of occupational commitment in the form of time and geographical flexibility (Barron and Norris, 1976; Garnsey, 1978). In many ways the growth of part-time employment for married women (Wainwright, 1978, p. 166) is indicative of this problem, because work for married women on a part- or full-time basis, does not by itself necessarily reduce their domestic burden or experience of socioeconomic dependence.

This is not to suggest that the professional worker/husband is bereft of problems in relation to home and work—rather, to emphasise that in the existing hierarchy of dependence, it is the breadwinning husband who tends to have the most direct and enduring relationship to the external economic division of labour and its rewards, and the homemaker wife who tends to have a more indirect and intermittent relationship to the same. Consequently, it is the husband who is the main link between the private world of the family and the public world of work and universalistic values; it is the husband who conveys the demands of that world to the family. It is the wife (and children) who largely depend upon the husband for sustenance; and it is therefore the wife who tends to 'accommodate' to the husband who in turn has to 'accommodate' to the occupational system. If the wife enters the world of work, she is subordinate in a distorted way in that sphere as well. The husband's position in the family could be said to be one of delegated power. Furthermore, whereas the husband's relationship to the external division of economic labour can be tempered by recourse to both individual and collective action, the wife's relationship to the household division of labour can only be moderated by the use of individual sanctions. To the extent that all married couples conform to the sex-based division of labour, they are likely to experience in varying degrees the associated structure of unequal relationships. Consequently, the professional worker and his wife is but one possibly distinct expression of a more generally felt hierarchy of dependence that is rooted in the contemporary bifurcation of society which equates women with domestic labour and men with paid work.

This structure of relationships is sustained and reinforced by a plethora of institutions and processes including education, the state, the media and above all the organisation of economic life.[1] The sexual division of labour in society and the family are therefore two sides of the same coin. The 'external' and 'internal' forms of this unequal sexual division of labour are mutually supportive. Men are obliged to work and therefore under the conditions of the prevailing socio-economic system are largely excluded from a major family role; women are obliged to work in the home and correspondingly are largely excluded from a major non-family role. In the context of marriage, the ideological forces that encourage and attempt to justify women's place in the home of necessity also have to prescribe paid work for men. Such a division of labour is predicated upon the twin primary social activities of economic production and the reproduction of labour power. Structural differentiation may have separated the two processes and over time they may have become excessively gender-based, but this cannot conceal the fact that man's disproportionate participation in the public sphere and woman's disproportionate participation in the private sphere are inextricably linked from the standpoint of marriage and family life in modern society.

Social theory and the family

Under the influence of certain social theorists, notably Parsons and

Goode, and to a lesser extent Litwak (1965), the conventional socio-logical understanding of this family and society relationship in the historically specific modern period is that the two systems 'fit' together quite neatly.[2] Thus, according to Parsons, the relatively isolated conjugal family is the one that 'interferes least with the functional needs of the occupational system' (1964, p. 192). In Parsons's work, functional needs refer mainly to the occupational and geographical mobility required by capital of 'free' wage labour. In addition to emphasising the ways in which the conjugal family 'fits' the 'needs' of the occupational system, Parsons also notes that at the same time the 'solidarity of the primary kinship unit', the conjugal family, is protected. In a manner reminiscent of Parsons, Goode claims that the characteristic traits of the conjugal family (that is, small, intense, independent, multilineal, neolocal, with a stress on the husband and wife relationship) 'fit rather well the demands of indus-trialisation' (1964, p. 108). Goode suggests that 'the needs of industrialisation' are for individuals who are not inhibited by exten-sive kinship obligations or by an ascriptive, kinship-based stratifica-tion system.

This is a familiar theme in many sociological textbooks.

The institutional emphasis on achievement rather than ascription, the competitiveness of the occupational system, the separation of home from work, and the existence of fairly well marked career patterns all make for a considerable amount of moving from one place to another. All these factors are compatible only with the type of family we have—the independent nuclear.

(Johnson, 1963, p. 245)

It can certainly be argued that the nuclear or conjugal family is a relatively good 'fit' with the needs of an industrial society. Indus-trialisation certainly requires a mobile labour force, and the result-ing geographical and social mobility will strain extended kinship ties.   (Cotgrove, 1972, p. 65)

The uncritical dissemination of the Parsons and Goode type of analy-sis fails to do justice to the complexity of their views and, more signifi-cantly, ignores the possibility that their version of the family-society equation may be faulty. For instance, Parsons is not unaware that the problems of reconciling the needs of the two systems produces 'strains' that in the main tend to be experienced more by women than men.

The feminine role is a conspicuous focus of the strains inherent in our social structure and not least of the sources of these strains is to be found in the functional difficulties in the integration of our kinship system with the rest of the social structure.

(Parsons, 1964, p. 194)

Thus, in a society in which the 'needs' of industry are paramount and the major source of power, wealth and prestige for most people is in an achieved occupation, women, of necessity as it were, are denied full equality. According to Parsons, women have to be excluded from the labour market except on the most disadvantageous of terms and allocated to occupational roles which tend to have a 'prominent expressive component' and/or 'are "supportive" of masculine roles' (Parsons, 1956, p. 15). All that remains for women in Parsons's model is the possibility of elaborating what in other respects Parsons designates a 'menial' job, namely, housework. Hence, Parsons talks about the option of a 'glamour' pattern and the 'professionalisation of the mother role', rather than about alternatives to an inequitable sexual division of labour.

Goode also notes that the family and industrial society relationship is problematic and, again like Parsons, writes that it is especially so for women. Among the 'disharmonies' that impinge on women, Goode suggests that in modern society women are 'given little relief' from domestic work including child-care and that they are more isolated socially than in the past (Goode, 1970, p. 15). Goode concludes that 'the "needs" of industrialisation are not in easy adjustment with the role obligations of women' (ibid., p. 17). Finally, Goode also suggests that the 'modern complex of industrialism and the conjugal family system' creates difficulties for the aged, the orphaned and the divorced, in addition to women (1964, pp. 109-10).

It is clear that Parsons and Goode both recognise that there are 'disharmonies' and that women in particular seem to be more oppressed than men by the separation of home from work and the association of women with responsibility for the former and men with responsibility for the latter. Yet they still both maintain that the conjugal family 'fits' best in some sense or senses the 'needs' of the industrial system. In the light of their own observations, such a conclusion would seem to be androcentric. They seem to regard the present situation as more or less inevitable and indicate an adherence to the assumption that the 'needs' of industry should be paramount and should take precedence over the 'needs' of all other institutions, including the family.

The thrust of the evidence and arguments advanced in this study suggest that from the point of view of individual family members, especially married women, the 'fit' between the family and the industrial economic system is a very imperfect one.[3] For example, it has been shown that in the case of the wives of professional workers, the various combinations of domestic work/paid work all involve significant social and economic costs. Data from other studies have also been widely quoted in support of this conclusion. For instance, one project on 'middle-class' couples concluded that 'the woman has to adapt more than her husband' (Pahl and Pahl, 1971, p. 235). In another study, extensive 'conflict' between work and family life was reported and found to be to the detriment of marriage in general and the wives in particular (Robertson, 1975).

Caplow, one of the few sociologists until recently to have examined housework as work, has gone so far as to suggest that, by the latter stages of their occupational career, housewives 'are the most conspicuously maladjusted segment of the population' (1964, p. 266). Morgan, although less directly concerned with housework, has also alluded briefly to the lack of 'fit' between the family and the world of work and the tendency for the resulting conflict to impinge more on women than men: 'The contradiction is felt particularly acutely by the woman but is not confined to her' (1975, p. 98). The separation and opposition between the family and the occupational system and its consequences have been well expressed by Harris: 'The estrangement from wider society of family households already small in size entails the social impoverishment of the women and children whose lives, by virtue of that estrangement, are centred within it' (1977, p. 79).

Thus it is difficult not to conclude that the current family and society structure of relationships considerably inconveniences wives more than husbands. What are often referred to as 'feminine dilemmas' (Myrdal and Klein, 1968, p. 135) are no more than reflections of the unresolved contradictory relationship between the family and the occupational system.

Neither Parsons nor Goode acknowledges that the ambiguous and generally disadvantageous situation of women in modern society is a major problem. Moreover, they both claim that the prevailing division of labour by sex is inevitable. Goode has written that it 'remains true that for women, the roles of wife and mother are their central obligations. For this reason, and because there is no one else who can be given the care of house and children, over the past half-century in the United States, women have not become much more "career minded" than they were, and polling evidence suggests that a similar conclusion may be applied to Europe' (1970, p. 16). As was indicated in Chapter 3, Parsons offers a somewhat more sophisticated biological and social explanation, though it is as unconvincing as Goode's.[4] Both kinds of explanations contain doubtful assumptions contributing to an inability, or even perhaps an unwillingness, to conceive of any alternative to the present situation in which the primary female role is located in the 'family' and the primary male role in 'society'. Thus, Parsons and Goode are essentially 'uncritical' sociologists; they tend to either accept or justify, rather than question the existing structure of society (Mills, 1967; Gouldner, 1971; Bottomore, 1975).

In contrast to Parsons and Goode, it can be argued that the 'maladjustment' of the family and women in modern society is compounded by the tendency to conceal the real value of domestic labour (Secombe, 1974; Oakley, 1976). The highly personal, unregulated and unpaid nature of housework sets it aside from 'real' work. Home and work are conventionally portrayed as opposites with the implication that household tasks do not conform to what is economically and culturally defined as 'work' in a society dominated by capital and the market.[5] Consequently, although domestic and child-care activities are crucial to the reproduction of labour power on a daily and generational basis and typically engage the housewife for many long and exacting hours, they are not rated as work.

According to this theory of the family and domestic labour in industrial capitalist societies (Secombe, 1973; Davidoff, 1976; Gardiner, 1976), plus the evidence already quoted from other studies, the predicament of the professional worker's wife is not unique. In a technical sampling sense, of course, it is not possible to generalise solely from the evidence of this study. However, to the extent that other couples conform to the husband/breadwinner and wife/homemaker models, their conjugal role relationships at the child-rearing stage of the family life-cycle are also likely to be segregated, unequal and husband-dominated. In other words, the subordination of the family to 'society', and therefore women to men, can take many forms. This is clearly demonstrated by Young and Willmott's more representative sample which included manual workers who worked shifts and managing directors who were almost totally absorbed in their work.

Following the completion of their researches, it is relatively unusual for sociologists to explicitly discuss the prescriptive implications of their findings. A notable and welcome exception to this convention is Oakley (1976). Oakley's research and therefore political emphasis is on the structure of essentially unequal relationships between men and women that in her view are supported and perpetuated by certain beliefs regarding a woman's place in the home. First, there is the belief that this division of labour by sex is 'natural, universal and necessary' (1976, p. 157). Secondly, there is the belief that women 'need to be mothers' and that children 'need' mothers (1976, p. 186). Oakley argues that these ideas are far from confirmed by comparative and historical evidence. Hence, they are myths that women should reject and they should also teach their children to reject them if the 'circle of learnt deprivation and induced subjugation is to be broken' (Oakley, 1976, p. 233).

However laudable, in the light of this study these recommendations are clearly insufficient. One cannot expect to change 'traditional' attitudes in advance of the conditions which gave rise to them. In other words, fundamental changes to the structure of work and family roles and their interrelationship are a prerequisite to ideological changes. Among other things, this means demanding what others have to some extent already achieved (Department of Employment, 1975); for example: nurseries for all throughout the year, compatibility of work schedules and the school day and year, maternity and paternity leave for all without prejudice, equal pay and equal entitlement to all state benefits including unemployment, social security and tax relief, and pay for workers who stay at home to look after children on a full-time basis or on the occasion of a child's ill-health. Whether or not any or all of these kinds of changes in the relationship between economic life and the family are fully attainable, given the continued pre-eminence of the competitive pursuit of profit, is doubtful. Certainly historical experience suggests that little will be achieved without a struggle, while contemporary evidence indicates that the predicament of married women is directly related to wider socioeconomic inequalities and contradictions (Brown and Harris, 1978).[6] Consequently, the demand for 'concessions' that in other respects may impair a 'society's' competitive position is unlikely to be well received.

In the meantime, it is also necessary to confirm and elaborate upon the findings of this particular study. This could include investigating a similar range of issues with other social groups as well as with a greater number and variety of professional workers and their wives. Moreover, it would be instructive to use different research methods, because different techniques, for example, case-study and survey methods, often produce different findings (Komarovsky, 1967, p. 348). By the same token, the work of Goffman (1959) and Berne (1969) suggests that some research designs are more effective than others at penetrating 'defensive' and 'protective' practices and the 'games that people play' in the presence of 'strangers'.

The role of the state, educational institutions, political parties, religious groups, the media, and so on, in relation to the nexus of unequal relationships described in this study have been far from fully researched. In particular, the ideological impact of the mass media, especially television, on what are currently regarded as appropriate male and female attitudes and behaviour patterns, would probably reveal that the implicit assumptions contained in most of the output are highly sexist.

Further research should also direct its attention to the sexual and physical dimensions of marriage. It may well be that the inclusion of material on, say, sexual bargaining and the threat and incidence of physical coercion within marriage, would necessitate modification of some of the conclusions presented in this study.

Finally, as far as the discussion of future research possibilities is concerned, if the 'irreducible base of family life as we know it is economic' (Turner, 1970, p. 263), the problem of the redistribution of income within the family remains a 'serious deficiency in our knowledge of our society' (Young, 1952, p. 305).

Whatever the subsequent direction and substance of commentary and research in this area, the following quotation, which was first published in 1949, succinctly expresses the central considerations of this study:

> Many young households give the impression of being on a basis of perfect equality. But as long as the man retains economic responsibility for the couple, this is only an illusion. It is he who decides where they will live, according to the demands of his work; she *follows* him from city to country or vice versa, to distant possessions, to foreign countries; their standard of living is set according to his income; the daily, weekly, annual rhythms are set by his occupation; associations and friendships most often depend upon his profession. Being more positively integrated in society than his wife, he guides the couple in intellectual, political and moral matters . . . the basic inequality still lies in the fact that the husband finds concrete self-realisation in work and action, whereas for the wife, as such, liberty has only a negative aspect.
>
> (de Beauvoir, 1972, pp. 498-9)

If the reader considers the conclusions of the present study unduly pessimistic, no comfort can be gained from a comparison between de Beauvoir's observations of approximately thirty years ago and the families described in this study. Despite de Beauvoir and other polemicists of her day, and the recrudescence of an extensive feminist and women's liberationist literature, public debate and agitation in recent years, little change was evident even in the consciousness of the couples studied. Neither husbands nor wives apparently felt even the need to pay lip service to egalitarian ideas, but boldly expressed their respective domination and subordination. Perhaps confronted by a highly inequitable social and economic system, this is a realistic appraisal of their situation. This consistency in norms and behaviour possibly represents an implicit rejection of certain fashionable yet inaccurate contemporary myths concerning marital equality.

Notes: Chapter 8

1 For a recent, though brief and uneven, summary of the forces and mechanisms which perpetuate the unequal sexual division of labour in modern Britain, see Wainwright (1978).

2 Litwak concentrates on the 'fit' between different types of extended kin relations and 'the demands of an industrial democratic society' (1965, p. 292). His notion of 'societal demands' is almost identical to those found in the works of Parsons and Goode. However, he is especially critical of Parsons's isolated nuclear family model and instead advances a modified extended family concept and concludes that through 'shared functioning' this type of family 'might be most effective in the maintenance of a democratic industrial society' (ibid., p. 323). For a critique of 'fit' theories see Harris (1969, pp. 93-121).

3 In general terms and from the standpoint of certain sociological traditions, notably those based on Marx and Veblen, the mass of sociological data on the alienating, dissatisfying, wasteful and unhealthy nature of most forms of work in industrial capitalist society testifies to the tendency to put the 'needs' of industry before the 'needs' of individuals (see, for example, Kapp, 1978).

4 For a critique of the 'myth of the division of labour by sex' aspect of Parsons's work, see Oakley (1976, pp. 178-85).

5 Braverman points out that 'hand and machine finish pressers, when employed by makers of clothing, are counted as manufacturing workers, but when employed by dry-cleaning plants they are workers in service industries' (1974, p. 361). I would add that when the same tasks are done in the home they cease to be work.

6 It is perhaps important to repeat that in no way is this meant to imply that the exploitation and oppression of women is unique to industrial capitalism, as Veblen (1899), among others, was fully aware.

APPENDIX 1

Research Methods

The full details of the research methods used in this study have been described elsewhere (Edgell, 1975). What follows, therefore, is very much a summary of the main points.

The research design adopted in this study facilitated the emergence of new ideas and their incorporation, and was in part selected for this reason. Consequently changes in orientation were anticipated, although not in the exact form that they took. Alternative research strategies, especially those that err on the side of verification, tend to be less flexible. However, no one methodology has a monopoly of advantages, there are always some disadvantages to be considered, and the presumed advantages/disadvantages are themselves open to question.

The decision to combine an exploratory approach with relatively intensive fieldwork techniques in a study of the conjugal role relationships of professional workers and their wives at the child-rearing stage of the family cycle was influenced by a number of factors.

An early consideration was the problem of privacy in family research. Textbooks and monographs on the sociology of the family rarely fail to mention the intimate character of family life and the difficulties this presents to those interested in studying this area. The problem is often expressed in the following way. The family is a primary group in which face-to-face interaction occurs between a small number of people related by blood/marriage and linked socially by such things as emotional attachment and economic exchange. However this 'unique' social formation is located in a society increasingly dominated by centralised capital and large-scale organisations that involve segmental, impersonal and instrumental relationships.[1] It is in this context that various researchers, including Bott (1971) and Rosser and Harris (1965), have observed that the private nature of family life represents one of the major obstacles to empirical research in this area. Consequently, the view that 'ever since sociology became an empirical subject, it has lived in the presence of the privacy of the persons it studied' (Shils, 1966, p. 299), is particularly relevant to family research. This is mainly because, in addition to the conventionally regarded private nature of family relationships in modern society,[2] access to a sample in this area often entails visiting respondents in their 'private' homes. Therefore fieldwork in family sociology can involve a double intrusion, into private relationships and private space. Adopting a research design in which a high response rate is not crucial to the success of the project was seen as one way of minimising some of the effects of the privacy problem. In short, I could 'risk' asking numerous and detailed questions without worrying too much about a high refusal rate.[3]

A second factor that influenced the choice of research methods concerns the lack of data bearing directly upon the issues that I wished to investigate. In fact the substantive theory which informed this research during the initial stages was based upon material extrapolated from at least four different areas of study.[4] Thus in the absence of well-established hypotheses, the survey method using a large random sample was thought inappropriate.

A further consideration favouring an exploratory research design was the complexity of the variables involved in conjugal role research. For example, Turner (1967) listed over ten factors that are relevant to the study of conjugal roles, many of which overlap and include other variables. The problem of complexity also applies to the dependent variables. As Platt (1969) and others have pointed out, degree of conjugal role segregation does not refer to a unidimensional aspect of marriage.

On balance, therefore, it was thought that the most appropriate research design would be one that involved a reasonably intensive study of a few families rather than a more superficial study of a large number of cases.

Spiralists were located with the co-operation of the Personnel Manager of a multinational company and a senior member of staff at a northern university. The project and its sampling requirements were explained with care and in detail and I was provided with lists of potential respondents who conformed to the category 'spiralist'. A pilot study of five couples was undertaken, the interview schedules and questionnaires were revised, and the pilot-stage couples re-interviewed. From this point onwards couples were selected with reference to a range of variables that were thought or known to be related to the patterning of conjugal roles.[5] Data collection and analysis proceeded together and consequently the findings partly influenced what data to collect next. Also an effort was made to gain the co-operation of less enthusiastic couples, for example, by writing to potential respondents several times. This strategy proved successful on many occasions.

The selection of respondents in terms of theoretical purpose and relevance has been called 'theoretical sampling' (Glaser and Strauss, 1968) and it introduces a greater element of control and flexibility into research. However, this study was not expressly formulated in relation to the general case for grounded theory. Any similarities between this project and the work of Glaser and Strauss derive from those aspects of grounded theory that were already established traditions in sociology,[6] and most important, recognition of the influence of Glaser and Strauss does not imply an uncritical acceptance of either their essentially interactionist position or their methodological prescriptions.

Eventually thirty-one scientists and engineers and their wives were investigated (twenty-four industrial scientists and seven academic scientists). Another group of less residentially mobile professional workers and their wives were interviewed to provide a contrast and to 'stretch' the 'diversity of the data as far as possible' (Glaser and Strauss, 1968, p. 61). What was needed was a small 'control' group of burgesses; in other words, a group of comparable professional workers who were linked to their local area by economic interests and who had no intention to change their employment status or move. Seven dentists were selected who all fulfilled these criteria, although one had recently changed from general practice to an administrative position within the same profession.

The main fieldwork techniques used in this study included the taped inter-view, questionnaires and, to a lesser extent, observational notes. Each couple were interviewed together and separately, the latter being achieved by asking one partner to complete a questionnaire in another room whilst the other was interviewed. The first interview with the couple together had the manifest purpose to gather basic demographic, life history, social network and other essentially factual data. Details of the interview schedules and questionnaires can be found in Appendix 2. The latent aim of the first interview was to encourage an atmosphere of confidence and establish rapport.

At the end of the first interview arrangements were made for the next. The taped material was transcribed in full the following day and observational notes were written up on such things as residential area, type of house, home conditions plus family (or any other) interaction. Points of particular interest or gaps in the data were also noted and raised at subsequent meetings. The separate interviews involved more detailed questions about home and work and lasted between one and three hours each. In a few exceptional cases the individual interviews lasted much longer and I was invariably asked a barrage of questions at the end of the data-collection session proper. In order to reduce the 'distance' (Galtung, 1970, p. 170) between the various research stages and generally ensure the reliability of the whole process, all the field-work was undertaken by the author.[7]

Data were eventually collected from thirty-eight couples at the child-rearing stage of the family cycle, although in two cases only the husband agreed to be interviewed. In one case the wife declined on grounds of ill-health. In the other, the wife objected in principle to social research. The sample was non-random and therefore no claim is made regarding the representativeness of those studied.

Notes: Appendix 1

1   See for example Komarovsky and Waller (1945), Hill (1958), Winch (1971) and Skolnick (1973).
2   For an interesting historical account of the division between public and private life and the political significance of this development, see Zaretsky (1976).
3   To disregard the problem of non-response even in a small project involving a non-random sample does not obviate the possibility of bias. In the event, second and third requests for co-operation were sent to potential respondents. This had the effect of drawing into the study those who were initially less than enthusiastic about participating and of increasing the response rate. However, gaining the co-operation of those near the apex of a bureaucratic hierarchy proved more difficult than gain-ing the co-operation of those nearer to the base. Consequently, the non-random sample is weighted towards the latter.
4   These are (1) general theories relating family patterns to types of society (Parsons, 1949, 1952 and 1956; Goode, 1970); (2) studies of contemporary family and kinship structures (Litwak, 1960a and 1960b; Willmott and Young, 1960; Blood and Wolfe, 1960; Bell, 1968a; Bott, 1971); (3) occupational sociology (Greenwood, 1957; Kornhauser, 1962; Blau and Duncan, 1967); (4) studies that cover linkages between two or more structurally differentiated areas of social life in the context of a com-munity study, occupational study, or a particular social process such as mobility (Mogey, 1956; McKinley, 1964; Glass, 1954).

5   For example, occupation, geographical and social mobility, ecological variables, education, stage of the family cycle, the employment of the wife outside the home. See also the lists and commentary by Bott (1971, p. 304) and Edgell (1970, pp. 317-18).

6   In certain respects the work of Bott (1971) represents a good example of grounded research but is not usually thought of in this light. For example, Bott did not set out with any established hypotheses in mind and the collection of data and the analysis of data stages proceeded together.

7   For a discussion of some of the problems of hiring research assistants to perform the more routine tasks, see Roth (1966).

APPENDIX 2

Interview Schedules and Questionnaire

(Final versions, that is, the range and form of the questions at the end of
the fieldwork)

First Interview—Husband and Wife Together

Background Information
1 Places and dates of birth of all household members.
2 Place and date of marriage.
3 Residence patterns of the husband and wife since birth.
4 Families of orientation—ages, marital status, locations, occupations.
5 Couple's educational background.
6 Couple's occupational background.
7 Social network(s)—relatives, friends, neighbours and colleagues—frequency and forms of contact, types of relationship, joint or separate, preferences.
8 Organisational membership—political, social, sport, educational, religious, professional, others. Who belongs to what, nature of involvement, preferences.
9 If you had more time would you see more people or join more organisations? Which people, which organisations?

Family Life
1 Weekday evenings at home—summer and winter.
2 Weekends—summer and winter.
3 Evenings and weekends out—frequency, alone or together, where to, preferences.
4 Babysitting problem (where relevant).
5 Typical Christmas and summer holidays.
6 Would you like more free time? (probe)
7 Extra holiday or pay? Inheritance/retirement/change of job, house, car, etc.
8 Other interests and activities—joint or separate.
9 Description of interest and participation in (a) child development, (b) cooking and (c) 'do-it-yourself'.

Second Interview—Husband Only

Work Career

1 Present occupation—grade and job description.
2 Length of time in present job and position.
3 Other jobs since entering labour market—company, length of service, job description, promotion, reason for leaving.
4 Did any of your occupational changes involve moving? (probe for details)
5 Own and wife's attitude towards job changes and moving (conflict?)
6 Comparison of present job and position with all other jobs/positions—probe for details concerning money, status, work interest, conditions, promotion prospects, etc.
7 Job and occupational position would *like* to have in (a) five years' time, (b) ten years' time and (c) at retirement.
8 Job and occupational position *expect* to have in (a) five years' time, (b) ten years' time and (c) at retirement.
9 Do you intend changing your job in the near or distant future? (probe for reasons)
10 When you think about changing or not changing your job, what kinds of things do you consider most? (probe for details of priorities, work career, family, environments, etc.)
11 What in your opinion constitutes a successful career in your field?
12 (Card 1) In terms of the following factors and categories, how successful would you say you have been in your career up to the present time? Very successful, successful, relatively unsuccessful.
   (a) Salary
   (b) Administrative responsibility
   (c) Professional recognition
   (d) Personal satisfaction
   (e) Material acquisitions
   (f) Power within the organisation
   (g) Recognition from your employer
   (h) Work enjoyment
13 Do you think that you have been more or less occupationally successful than your father/brothers/sisters/friends/colleagues/neighbours?
14 Whose opinion do you care about most? (probe—work and non-work)
15 If you could start all over again, would you enter the same professional career? (probe)
16 What is most important to you, advancement in the organisation or professional recognition? (or neither)
17 Courses, conferences, business trips, work late (at home and at work). Frequency, attitude towards, wife's attitude.

Family Life

1 What time do you get home from work most evenings?
2 Do you ever bring work home? (details)
3 What is your wife's attitude to you working at home or late at the office? (probe)

4 How often do you discuss your work with your wife?
5 What aspects of your work does your wife ask about?
6 Does your wife understand very much about your work?
7 How much interest, would you say, does she take in your work career?
8 What aspects of your work does she find most interesting and what aspects does she dislike?
9 (Card 2) There are many different ideas about how 'important' family decisions ought to be made. What is true for you in your experience and what would you like to be true?
   (a) The husband decides without consulting his wife.
   (b) The husband decides after consulting his wife.
   (c) The husband and wife decide together.
   (d) The wife decides after consulting her husband.
   (e) The wife decides without consulting her husband.
10 What decisions are 'important' may not be the same for everybody. (Card 3) How important are the following decisions in your opinion and how are they made in your family?
   (a) Domestic spending. Very important, just important, not important.
   (b) Holidays.
   (c) Children's education.
   (d) Buying a house.
   (e) Buying a car.
11 Since you were married, what are the main things you have disagreed about? (probe—money, sex, in-laws, time, activities)
12 How successful do you consider your marriage to be?
13 How would you judge the 'success' of marriage? (probe for details on conjugal role models and expectations)
14 If you have had a 'bad' day at work, do you ever mention it to your wife? (probe for details, including wife's reaction)
15 If your wife ever has a 'bad' day, does she mention it to you?
16 What is your view of women who work outside the home?
17 Who do you spend most of your non-work time with?
18 What kinds of jobs would you like your children to have? (sons, daughters)
19 If you were offered a 'better' job, but your wife did not want to move because of her social life, what would you do? (same again with children's education)
20 (Card 4) Thinking of your work, your home and family life, and your leisure interests and activities, which do you consider the most enjoyable, interesting, worry about most, find most rewarding/important?
21 Finally, are there any ways in which your work life affects your home life (and vice versa) that we have not discussed?

Third Interview—Wife Only

Work Career
1 What was your last full-time job?
2 How long were you in this job? Details—promotion, salary, work

interest, satisfaction, enjoyment, etc.
3   Why did you stop work? (if applicable)
(If applicable)
4   Present occupation—grade and job description.
5   Length of time in present job and position.
6   Whose idea was it that you should return to work?
7   What do you consider are the benefits and disadvantages of working outside the home?
8   What do you most like about your present job? (details—hours, conditions, work interest, status, salary, satisfaction, etc.)
(If applicable)
9   Do you have any desire to return to work? (part-time/full-time)
10 Why? (probe for details of motives, and reasons for particular work)
11 Does your husband want you to return to work? (full-time/part-time)
12 If you never intend to return to work outside the home, what are your attitudes towards married women who work, and work in general? (probe)

Family Life

1   Would you describe to me a typical weekday at home? (probe)
2   Are you ever bored at home? (probe—domestic help?)
3   (Card 2) There are many different ideas about how 'important' family decisions ought to be made. What is true in your experience and what would you like to be true?
   (a)   The husband decides without consulting his wife.
   (b)   The husband decides after consulting his wife.
   (c)   The husband and wife decide together.
   (d)   The wife decides after consulting her husband.
   (e)   The wife decides without consulting her husband.
4   What decisions are 'important' may not be the same for everybody. (Card 3) How important are the following decisions in your opinion and how are they made in your family?
   (a)   Domestic spending. Very important, just important, not important.
   (b)   Holidays.
   (c)   Children's education.
   (d)   Buying a house.
   (e)   Buying a car.
5   Since you were married what are the main things you have disagreed about? (probe—money, sex, in-laws, time, activities)
6   How successful do you consider your marriage to be?
7   How would you judge the 'success' of marriage? (probe for details on conjugal role models and expectations)
8   If you have a 'bad' day at home/work, do you ever mention it to your husband? (probe)
9   If your husband ever has a 'bad' day at work, does he ever mention it to you?
10 If you were given an extra four hours each day, how would you spend it? (probe)
11 Do you ever discuss your 'work' or your husband's work with him?

12   What aspect of his work do you find most interesting?
13   What is your attitude towards your husband working at home, working late, going on courses, etc? (probe)
14   Do you miss or regret not having a career like your husband? (probe)
15   What kind of jobs would you like your children to have? (sons, daughters)
16   Who do you spend most of your non-work (domestic or otherwise) time with?
17   (Card 4) Thinking of your work (domestic or otherwise), home and family life, and leisure interests and activities, which do you consider the most enjoyable, interesting, worry about most, find most rewarding/ important?

Observational Notes

1   Neighbourhood
2   House and contents
3   Husband and wife interaction and domestic behaviour
4   Parent and child interaction
5   Questions about the project and motives for taking part

Questionnaire

Professional Families Survey: Confidential

The following are simple 'who does what?' questions. In every family there are many ways of dividing up tasks and responsibilities, so there are no right or wrong answers since there is no one 'correct' way of dividing up these things. Needless to say, I want to know who actually does what and not who ought to do what. Please try and answer each question and if in doubt about a question leave it, complete the form and ask at the end.

TASK Who...	Husband always	Husband mostly	Husband and wife equally	Wife mostly	Wife always	Neither (please state who)
(1) gets up first in morning?						
(2) cooks breakfast?						
(3) cooks evening meal?						
(4) prepares snacks?						
(5) cleans the car?						

(6) cleans
the house?
(7) washes up?
(8) wipes up?
(9) tidies up?
(10) maintains
car?
(11) maintains
the house?
(12) maintains
garden?
(13) dresses
the children?
(14) plays with
them?
(15) corrects
their
behaviour?
(16) baths
them at
night?
(17) keeps
track of
money and
bills?
(18) decides
when to
buy a
new car?
(19) decides
when to
buy new
furniture?
(20) decides what
to do at
weekends?
(21) decides
where to
go on
holiday?
(22) chooses
the child-
ren's clothes?
(23) chooses
interior
decorations?
(24) decides
who to
entertain?

(25) decides
what film/
play to see?
(26) does the
shopping?
(27) does the
laundry?
(28) drives
the car?

---

1 In our society some people claim that equality between the sexes has been achieved. Do you agree? ....

2 Would you briefly explain why you agree or disagree in Question 1 above
....
....
....

3 Do you think that equality between the sexes in all walks of life is a good thing or a bad thing? ....

4 Would you briefly explain why you think that equality between the sexes is a good or bad thing? ....
....
....

5 How do you regard domesticity? Please delete any inappropriate words. Easy/difficult/boring/interesting/worthwhile/waste of time/enjoyable/ unenjoyable/satisfying/unsatisfying.

6 Whose company do you prefer most? Please delete any inappropriate words. Relatives/friends/professional colleagues/males/females.

7 If you were granted three wishes, what would you wish for? Please be as specific as possible and put them in order of importance.
(a) ....
(b) ....
(c) ....

Please try and answer all the following questions as frankly as possible. This is of the highest importance if the survey findings are to be valid. There are no 'right' or 'wrong' answers. Please indicate your answers by marking the response which most accurately fits your own experience.

1a Do you and your mate agree on how your children should be brought up? Always agree/almost always agree/occasionally agree/occasionally disagree/almost always disagree/always disagree.

2a Do you and your mate agree on the type of education your children should receive?
Always agree/almost always agree/occasionally agree/occasionally disagree/almost always disagree/always disagree.

3a Do you and your mate agree on the subject of contraception?
Always agree/almost always agree/occasionally agree/occasionally disagree/almost always disagree/always disagree.

4b Do you and your mate agree on the demonstration of affection?

Always agree/almost always agree/occasionally agree/occasionally disagree/almost always disagree/always disagree.

5b How often do you and your mate get on each other's nerves around the house?
Never/sometimes/frequently.

6b Which of the following items have caused difficulties in your marriage?

Children:	None	Major difficulties	Minor difficulties
Money:	None	Major difficulties	Minor difficulties
Interference from in-laws:	None	Major difficulties	Minor difficulties
Selfishness:	None	Major difficulties	Minor difficulties
Lack of mutual affection:	None	Major difficulties	Minor difficulties
Unsatisfying sexual relations:	None	Major difficulties	Minor difficulties

7c Do you and your mate agree on family finances?
Always agree/almost always agree/occasionally agree/occasionally disagree/almost always disagree/always disagree.

8c Do you and your mate agree on how much money should be spent on the following items? (In this and some later questions please put a tick instead of underlining your answer.)

	House	Children	Car	Leisure	Holidays
Always agree					
Almost always agree					
Occasionally agree					
Occasionally disagree					
Almost always disagree					
Always disagree					

9c Do you and your mate agree on how much money should be saved, invested, put into insurance?

	Saved	Invested	Insurance
Always agree			
Almost always agree			
Occasionally agree			
Occasionally disagree			
Almost always disagree			
Always disagree			

10c When disagreements arise over money matters what usually happens?
Husband gives in/wife gives in/neither gives in/agreement by mutual consent.

11d Do you and your mate agree on what you consider to be 'good', 'correct' behaviour of each other?
Always agree/almost always agree/occasionally agree/occasionally disagree/almost always disagree/always disagree.

12d Do you and your mate agree on the amount of time you spend together?
Always agree/almost always agree/occasionally agree/occasionally disagree/almost always disagree/always disagree.

13d Do you and your mate engage in activities and interests together?

	Outside the home	Inside the home
All		
Some		
Few		
None		

14d Do you and your mate agree on friends?
Always agree/almost always agree/occasionally agree/occasionally disagree/almost always disagree/always disagree.

15d When disagreements arise in matters other than financial and sexual what is the general result?
Husband gives in/wife gives in/neither gives in/agreement by mutual consent.

16e Do you and your mate agree on how often you should have sexual relations?
Always agree/almost always agree/occasionally agree/occasionally disagree/almost always disagree/always disagree.

17e Are sexual relations between you and your mate an expression of love and affection?
Always/almost always/sometimes/almost never/never.

18e What are your feelings on sexual relations with your mate?
Very enjoyable/enjoyable/satisfactory/unsatisfactory/unenjoyable.

19e When disagreements arise in sexual matters what is the general result?
Husband gives in/wife gives in/neither gives in/agreement by mutual consent.

20f Have you ever wished you had not married or had not had children?

	Not married	Not had children
Frequently		
Occasionally		
Rarely		
Never		

21f How happy would you rate your marriage?
Very happy/happy/average/unhappy/very unhappy.

22f If you had your life over again would you:

    (a)   Marry the same person? _____
    (b)   Marry a different person? _____
    (c)   Not marry at all? _____

23f   Have you and your mate ever parted because of conflict?
      Never/once/more than once.
      If once or more than once, what was the conflict over?
      ....

24f   Have you ever thought of parting?
      Frequently/occasionally/rarely/never.

Thank you once more for your co-operation in this research.

Main Characteristics of the Sample

1 Sex

Husbands	38
Wives	36
Total	74

2 Age

	Husbands	Wives
25-30	8	8
31-35	5	6
36-40	10	15
41-45	9	6
46-50	4	2
51-55	2	1
	38	38

3 Number of Children

	Families
One child	7
Two children	16
Three children	10
Four children	2
Five children	1
Six children	1
Seven children	1
	38

4 Occupation

	Husbands
Scientists/engineers in industry	24
Scientists/engineers in university	7
Self-employed dentists	6
Medical administrator	1
	38

	Wives	
Full-time mothers/housewives	29	
Employed part-time outside the home	6	(including 4 teachers)
Employed full-time outside the home	3	(including 2 teachers)
	38	

The Occupational Status Scale used in This Study

The main considerations that led to the adoption of the occupational classification are described elsewhere (Edgell, 1975). The scale is the same one that was developed for and subsequently used in the 'affluent worker' project (Goldthorpe *et al.*, 1969, pp. 196-7).

Table A4.1   *Occupational Status Scale*

Occupational Status		Examples	Summary
1(a)	Higher professional and managerial employees	Scientists, dentists and university teachers	
(b)	Large-scale employers	—	
2(a)	Intermediate professional and managerial employees	Non-graduate teachers	'white collar'
(b)	Medium-scale employers	—	
3(a)	Lower professional and managerial employees	Wages clerk	
(b)	Small-scale employers	Shopkeepers	
4(a)	Supervisory, inspectional, minor officials and service employees	Foreman	'intermediate'
(b)	Self-employed individuals		
5	Skilled manual workers (apprenticeship or equivalent)	—	
6	Other relatively skilled manual workers	—	'manual'
7	Semi-skilled manual workers	—	
8	Unskilled manual workers	—	

Bibliography

Adorno, T. W. (1967), *Prisms* (London: Spearman).

Babchuk, N. and Bates, A. P. (1963), 'The primary relations of middle-class couples: a study in male dominance', *American Sociological Review*, vol. 28, pp. 377-84.

Banks, J. A. and Banks, O. (1964), 'Feminism and social change—a case study of a movement', in *Explorations in Social Change*, ed. G. K. Zollschan and W. Hirsch (London: Routledge & Kegan Paul), pp. 547-69.

Barker, D. and Allen, S. (eds) (1976a), *Sexual Divisions and Society: Process and Change* (London: Tavistock).

Barker, D. and Allen, S. (eds) (1976b), *Dependence and Exploitation in Work and Marriage* (London: Longman).

Barron, R. D. and Norris, G. M. (1976), 'Sexual divisions and the dual labour market', in *Dependence and Exploitation in Work and Marriage*, ed. D. Barker and S. Allen (1976b) (London: Longman), pp. 47-69.

Bell, C. R. (1968a), *Middle Class Families* (London: Routledge & Kegan Paul).

Bell, C. R. (1968b), 'Mobility and the middle class extended family', *Sociology*, vol. 2, pp. 173-84.

Bell, C. (1971), 'Occupational career, family cycle and extended family relations', *Human Relations*, vol. 24, pp. 463-75.

Bell, C. (1974), 'Review symposium', *Sociology*, vol. 8, pp. 505-7.

Bell, C. and Newby, H. (1976), 'Husbands and wives: dynamics of the deferential dialectic', in *Dependence and Exploitation in Work and Marriage*, eds D. Barker and S. Allen (1976b) (London: Longman), pp. 152-68.

Bernard, J. (1973), *The Future of Marriage* (London: Souvenir Press).

Berne, E. (1969), *The Games People Play*, (Harmondsworth: Penguin).

Blau, P. M. and Duncan, O. T. (1967), *The American Occupational Structure* (New York: Wiley).

Blood, R. O. and Wolfe, D. M. (1960), *Husbands and Wives* (London: Collier Macmillan).

Bott, E. (1971), *Family and Social Network* (London: Tavistock).

Bottomore, T. B. (1975), *Sociology as Social Criticism* (London: Allen & Unwin).

Braverman, H. (1974), *Labour and Monopoly Capital* (London: Monthly Review Press).

Brown, G. W. and Harris, T. (1978), *The Social Origins of Depression: A Study of Psychiatric Disorder in Women* (London: Tavistock).

Burgess, E. W., Locke, H. J. and Thomes, M. M. (1963), *The Family* (New York: American Book Co.).

Caplow, T. (1964), *The Sociology of Work* (London: McGraw-Hill).

Castles, S. and Kosack, G. (1973), *Immigrant Workers and Class Structure in Western Europe* (London: Oxford University Press).

Central Statistical Office (1974), *Social Trends*, no. 5 (London: HMSO).

Christensen, H. T. (ed.) (1964), *Handbook of Marriage and the Family* (Chicago: Rand McNally).

Cohen, G. (1977), 'Absentee husbands in spiralist families', *Journal of Marriage and the Family*, vol. 39, pp. 595-604.

Cotgrove, S. F. (1972), *The Science of Society* (London: Allen & Unwin).

Cotgrove, S. and Box, S. (1970), *Science, Industry and Society* (London: Allen & Unwin).

Coulson, M., Magas, B. and Wainwright, H. (1975), 'The housewife and her labour under capitalism—a critique', *New Left Review*, vol. 89, pp. 59-72.

Counter Information Services (1976), *Women Under Attack* (London: Counter Information Services).

Coussins, J. (1977), *The Equality Report* (London: NCL Rights for Women Unit).

Cromwell, R. E. and Olson, D. H. (eds) (1975), *Power in Families* (New York: Sage).

Dahlstrom, E. (ed.) (1967), *The Changing Roles of Men and Women* (London: Duckworth).

Davidoff, L. (1976), 'The Rationalisation of Housework', in *Dependence and Exploitation in Work and Marriage*, ed. D. Barker and S. Allen (1976b) (London: Longman), pp. 121-51.

de Beauvoir, S. (1972), *The Second Sex* (Harmondsworth: Penguin).

de Grazia, S. (1962), *Of Time, Work and Leisure* (New York: Twentieth Century Fund).

Dennis, N. (1962), 'Secondary group relationships and the pre-eminence of the family', *International Journal of Comparative Sociology*, vol. 3, pp. 80-90.

Denzin, N. K. (1970), *The Research Act in Sociology* (London: Butterworth).

Department of Employment (1975), *Women and Work*, Manpower Paper No. 12 (London: HMSO).

Dubin, R. (1956), 'Industrial workers' worlds: a study of the central life interest of industrial workers', *Social Problems*, vol. 3, pp. 131-42.

Dumazedier, J. (1967), *Toward a Society of Leisure* (London: Collier Macmillan).

Eccles, J. D. and Powell, M. (1967), 'The health of dentists: a survey in South Wales', *British Dental Journal*, vol. 123, pp. 379-87.

Edgell, S. R. (1970), 'Spiralists: their careers and family lives', *British Journal of Sociology*, vol. 21, pp. 314-23.

Edgell, S. R. (1975), 'Conjugal role relationships among professional workers and their wives at the child-rearing stage of the family life cycle', unpublished PhD thesis, University of Salford.

Elliott, P. (1972), *The Sociology of the Professions* (London: Macmillan).

Engels, F. (1962), 'The condition of the working-class in England', in *On Britain*, K. Marx and F. Engels (Moscow: Foreign Languages Publishing House), pp. 3-338.

Engels, F. (1972), *The Origin of the Family, Private Property and the State* (London: Lawrence & Wishart).

Equal Opportunities Commission (1978a), *Second Annual Report: 1977* (London: HMSO).

Equal Opportunities Commission (1978b), *Equality Between the Sexes in Industry* (Manchester: Equal Opportunities Commission).

Eysenck, H. J. (1962), *Uses and Abuses of Psychology* (Harmondsworth: Penguin).

Finer Report (1974), *One Parent Families*, Vol. 1, Cmnd 5629 (London: HMSO).

Firth, R., Hubert, J. and Forge, A. (1969), *Families and their Relatives* (London: Routledge & Kegan Paul).

Fletcher, R. (1962), *The Family and Marriage* (Harmondsworth: Penguin).

Fogarty, M., Rapoport, R. and Rapoport, R. N. (1971), *Sex, Career and Family* (London: Allen & Unwin).

Foote, N. N. (ed.) (1969), 'Household Decision-making', *Consumer Behaviour*, vol. 4 (New York: NY University Press).

Ford, J. and Box, S. (1967), 'Sociological theory and occupational choice', *Sociological Review*, vol. 15, pp. 287-309.

Galtung, J. (1970), *Theory and Methods of Social Research* (London: Allen & Unwin).

Gardiner, J. (1975), 'Women's domestic labour', *New Left Review*, vol. 89, pp. 47-58.

Gardiner, J. (1976), 'Political economy of domestic labour in capitalist society', in *Dependence and Exploitation in Work and Marriage*, ed. D. Barker and S. Allen (1976b) (London: Longman), pp. 109-20.

Garnsey, E. (1978), 'Women's work and theories of class stratification', *Sociology*, vol. 12, pp. 223-43.

Gavron, H. (1966), *The Captive Wife* (Harmondsworth: Penguin).

Gerstl, J. E. and Hutton, S. P. (1966), *Engineers: The Anatomy of a Profession* (London: Tavistock).

Gillespie, D. L. (1971), 'Who has the power? The marital struggle', *Journal of Marriage and the Family*, vol. 33, pp. 445-58.

Glaser, B. G. and Strauss, A. L. (1968), *The Discovery of Grounded Theory* (London: Weidenfeld & Nicolson).

Glass, D. V. (ed.) (1954), *Social Mobility in Britain* (London: Routledge & Kegan Paul).

Glick, P. C. and Parke, R. (1965), 'New approaches in studying the life cycle of the family', *Demography*, vol. 2, pp. 187-202.

Goffman, E. (1959), *The Presentation of Self in Everyday Life* (New York: Doubleday/Anchor).

Goffman, E. (1968), *Asylums* (Harmondsworth: Penguin).

Goffman, E. (1977), 'The arrangement between the sexes', *Theory and Society*, vol. 4, pp. 301-31.

Goldthorpe, J. H., Lockwood, D., Bechhofer, F. and Platt, J. (1968), *The Affluent Worker: Industrial Attitudes and Behaviour* (Cambridge: Cambridge University Press).

Goldthorpe, J. H., Lockwood, D., Bechhofer, F. and Platt, J. (1969), *The Affluent Worker in the Class Structure* (Cambridge: Cambridge University Press).

Goode, W. J. (1964), *The Family* (Englewood Cliffs, NJ: Prentice-Hall).

Goode, W. J. (1970), *World Revolution and Family Patterns* (London: Collier Macmillan).

Gouldner, A. (1971), *The Coming Crisis of Western Sociology* (London: Heinemann).

Greenwood, E. (1957), 'Attributes of a profession', *Social Work*, vol. 2, pp. 44-55.

Gross, E. (1958), *Work and Society* (New York: Cromwell).

Hamilton, R. (1978), *The Liberation of Women* (London: Allen & Unwin).

Hammond, S. B. and Oeser, O. A. (1954), *Social Structure and Personality in a City* (London: Routledge & Kegan Paul).

Harrell-Bond, B. (1969), 'Conjugal role behaviour', *Human Relations*, vol. 22, pp. 77-91.

Harris, C. C. (1969), *The Family* (London: Allen & Unwin).

Harris, C. C. (ed.) (1970), *Readings in Kinship in Urban Society* (Oxford: Pergamon Press).

Harris, C. C. (1977), 'Changing conceptions of the relation between family and societal form in Western society' in *Industrial Society: Class Cleavage and Control*, ed. R. Scase (London: Allen & Unwin), pp. 74-89.

Hart, M. N. (1973), 'Adjustment to marital breakdown', unpublished PhD thesis, University of East Anglia.

Hill, R. (1958), 'Sociology of marriage and family behaviour', *Current Sociology*, vol. 7, pp. 1-98.

Hillman, M. and Whalley, A. (1977), 'Fair play for all: a study of access to sport and informal recreation', *Political and Economic Planning*, vol. XLIII, Broadsheet No. 571.

Hirsch, W. (1968), *Scientists in American Society* (New York: Random House).

Hobson, D. (1978), 'Housewives: isolation as oppression' in *Women Take Issue: Aspects of Women's Subordination*, Women's Study Group, Centre for Contemporary Cultural Studies, University of Birmingham (London: Hutchinson), pp. 79-95.

Holmstrom, L. L. (1972), *The Two Career Family* (Cambridge, Mass.: Schenkman).

Holter, H. (1970), *Sex Roles and Social Structure* (Oslo: Universitet-Forlaget).

Horoszowski, P. (1971a), 'Woman's status in socialistic and capitalistic countries (I)', *International Journal of Sociology of the Family*, vol. 1, pp. 35-52.

Horoszowski, P. (1971b), 'Woman's status in socialistic and capitalistic countries (II)', *International Journal of Sociology of the Family*, vol. 1, pp. 160-80.

Hunt, A. (1968), *A Survey of Women's Employment* (London: HMSO).

Jackson, J. A. (1969), *Migration* (Cambridge: Cambridge University Press).

Jahoda, M., Lazarsfeld, P. F. and Zeisel, H. (1972), *Marienthal: The Sociology of an Unemployed Community* (London: Tavistock).

Jansen, C. J. (1968), 'Social aspects of internal migration: a research report' (mimeo.) (Bath).

Jansen, C. J. (1970), *Readings in the Sociology of Migration* (Oxford: Pergamon Press).

Johnson, H. M. (1963), *Sociology: A Systematic Introduction* (London: Routledge & Kegan Paul).

Kapp, K. W. (1978), *The Social Costs of Business Enterprise* (Nottingham: Spokesman).

Klein, J. (1965), *Samples from English Cultures*, Vols 1 and 2 (London: Routledge & Kegan Paul).

Komarovsky, M. (1967), *Blue-Collar Marriage* (New York: Random House).

Komarovsky, M. and Waller, W. (1945), 'Studies of the family', *American Journal of Sociology*, vol. 50, pp. 443-51.

Kornhauser, W. (1962), *Scientists in Industry* (Berkeley, Calif.: University of California Press).

Land, H. (1976), 'Women: supporters or supported', in *Sexual Divisions and Society: Process and Change*, ed. D. Barker and S. Allen (1976a) (London: Tavistock), pp. 108-32.

Lane, M. (1972), 'Explaining educational choice', *Sociology*, vol. 6, pp. 255-66.

Litwak, E. (1960a), 'Occupational mobility and extended family cohesion', *American Sociological Review*, vol. 25, pp. 9-21.

Litwak, E. (1960b), 'Geographic mobility and extended family cohesion', *American Sociological Review*, vol. 25, pp. 385-94.

Litwak, E. (1965), 'Extended kin relations in an industrial democratic society', in *Social Structure and the Family*, ed. E. Shanas and G. F. Streib (Englewood Cliffs, NJ: Prentice Hall), pp. 290-323.

Long, L. H. (1974), 'Women's labour force participation and the residential mobility of families', *Social Forces*, vol. 52, pp. 342-8.

Lopata, H. Z. (1972), *Occupation: Housewife* (London: Oxford University Press).

Mackie, L. and Pattullo, P. (1977), *Women at Work* (London: Tavistock).

Marsden, D. and Duff, E. (1975), *Workless: Some Unemployed Men and their Families* (Harmondsworth: Penguin).

Marx, K. (1970), *Capital*, Vol. I (London: Lawrence & Wishart).

Meissner, M. (1977), 'Sexual division of labour and inequality: labour and leisure', in *Women in Canada*, ed. M. Stephenson (Ontario: General Publishing), pp. 160-80.

Middleton, C. (1974), 'Sexual inequality and stratification theory', in *The Social Analysis of Class Structure*, ed. F. Parkin (1974) (London: Tavistock), pp. 180-203.

Mills, C. W. (1956), *White Collar* (New York: Oxford University Press).

Mills, C. W. (1967), *The Sociological Imagination* (London: Oxford University Press).

Mitchell, J. (1974), *Women's Estate* (Harmondsworth: Penguin).

Mogey, J. M. (1956), *Family and Neighbourhood* (London: Oxford University Press).

Morgan, D. H. J. (1975), *Social Theory and the Family* (London: Routledge & Kegan Paul).

Morse, N. C. and Weiss, R. S. (1955), 'The function and meaning of work and the job', *American Sociological Review*, vol. 20, pp. 191-8.

Musgrave, P. (1967), 'Towards a theory of occupational choice', *Sociological Review*, vol. 15, pp. 33-46.

Myrdal, A. and Klein, V. (1968), *Women's Two Roles* (London: Routledge & Kegan Paul).

McCall, G. and Simmons, J. (1966), *Identities and Interactions* (New York: Free Press).

McKinley, D. G. (1964), *Social Class and Family Life* (London: Collier Macmillan).

Nandy, L. and Nandy, D. (1975), 'Towards true equality for women', *New Society*, vol. 31, pp. 246-9.

Newson, J. and Newson, E. (1963), *Patterns of Infant Care* (Harmondsworth: Penguin).

Nisbet, R. (1970), *The Social Bond* (New York: Alfred Knopf).

Nye, F. I. and Hoffman, L. W. (eds) (1965), *The Employed Mother in America* (Chicago: Rand McNally).

Oakley, A. (1974), *The Sociology of Housework* (London: Martin Robertson).

Oakley, A. (1976), *Housewife* (Harmondsworth: Penguin).

Ogburn, W. F. and Nimkoff, M. F. (1955), *Technology and the Changing Family* (Cambridge, Mass.: Houghton Mifflin).

Oppong, C. (1975), 'A note on attitudes to jointness of the conjugal role relationship and family size: a study of norms among Ghanaian students', *Human Relations*, vol. 28, pp. 801-9.

Orzack, L. H. (1959), 'The idea of work as a central life interest of professionals', *Social Problems*, vol. 7, pp. 125-32.

Pahl, J. M. and Pahl, R. E. (1971), *Managers and Their Wives* (London: Allen Lane).

Parker, S. R. (1971), 'Work and leisure' in *The Sociology of Industry*, ed. S. R. Parker, R. K. Brown, J. Child and M. A. Smith (1971) (London: Allen & Unwin), pp. 173-81.

Parker, S. (1972), *The Future of Work and Leisure* (London: Paladin).

Parker, S. (1973), 'Relations between work and leisure', in *Leisure and Society in Britain*, ed. M. A. Smith, S. Parker and C. Smith (London: Allen Lane).

Parker, S. (1976), *The Sociology of Leisure* (London: Allen & Unwin).

Parsons, T. (1949), The Social Structure of the Family', in *The Family: Its Function and Destiny*, ed. R. N. Anshen (New York: Harper & Row).

Parsons, T. (1952), *The Social System* (London: Routledge & Kegan Paul).

Parsons, T. (1956), *Family, Socialisation and Interaction Process* (London: Routledge & Kegan Paul).

Parsons, T. (1964), *Essays in Sociological Theory* (New York: Free Press).

Platt, J. (1969), 'Some problems of measuring the jointness of conjugal role relationships', *Sociology*, vol. 3, pp. 287-97.

Presthus, R. (1962), *The Organizational Society* (New York: Random House).

Rapoport, R. and Rapoport, R. N. (1971), *Dual-Career Families* (Harmondsworth: Penguin).

Rapoport, R. and Rapoport, R. N. (1974), 'Four themes in the sociology of leisure', *British Journal of Sociology*, vol. 25, pp. 215-29.

Roberts, K. (1970), *Leisure* (London: Longman).

Roberts, K., Cook, F. G., Clark, S. C. and Semeonoff, E. (1976), 'The family life cycle, domestic roles and the meaning of leisure', *Society and Leisure*, vol. 8, pp. 7-20.

Robertson, F. (1975), 'Work and the conjugal family: a study of the inter-relationship between work and family in the life interests of hospital doctors and general dental practitioners', unpublished PhD thesis, University of Edinburgh.

Rodgers, R. H. (1964), 'Some factors associated with homogeneous role patterns in family life cycle careers', *Pacific Sociological Review*, vol. 7, pp. 38-48.

Rose, A. M. (1958), 'Distance of migration and socio-economic status of migrants', *American Sociological Review*, vol. 23, pp. 420-3.

Rosow, I. (1967), *The Social Integration of the Aged* (New York: Collier Macmillan).

Rosser, C. and Harris, C. (1965), *The Family and Social Change* (London: Routledge & Kegan Paul).

Rossi, A. S. (1964), 'Equality between the sexes: an immodest proposal', *Daedalus*, vol. 93, pp. 607-52.

Roth, J. (1963), *Timetables* (Indianapolis, Ind.: Bobbs-Merrill).

Roth, J. (1966), 'Hired hand research', *American Sociologist*, vol. 1, pp. 190-6.

Routh, G. (1965), *Occupation and Pay in Great Britain 1906-1960* (Cambridge: Cambridge University Press).

Rowbotham, S. (1972), *Women's Liberation and Revolution: A Bibliography* (Bristol: Falling Wall Press).

Rowbotham, S. (1973), *Women's Consciousness, Man's World* (Harmondsworth: Penguin).

Rowbotham, S. (1974), *Hidden from History* (London: Pluto Press).

Rowe, G. P. (1966), 'The developmental conceptual framework to the study of the family' in *Emerging Conceptual Frameworks in Family Analysis*, ed. F. I. Nye and F. M. Berado (London: Collier Macmillan), pp. 198-222.

Safilios-Rothschild, C. (1969), 'Family sociology or wives' family sociology', *Journal of Marriage and the Family*, vol. 31, pp. 290-301.

Safilios-Rothschild, C. (1970a), 'The influence of the wife's degree of work commitment upon some aspects of family organisation and dynamics', *Journal of Marriage and the Family*, vol. 32, pp. 681-91.

Safilios-Rothschild, C. (1970b), 'The study of family power structure: a review 1960-1969', *Journal of Marriage and the Family*, vol. 32, pp. 539-52.

Safilios-Rothschild, C. (1976), 'A macro- and micro-examination of power and love: an exchange model', *Journal of Marriage and the Family*, vol. 38, pp. 355-64.

Salvo, V. J. (1969), 'Familial and occupational roles in a technological society', in *The Engineers and the Social System*, ed. R. Perrucci and J. E. Gerstl (London: Wiley), pp. 311-34.

Secombe, W. (1973), 'The housewife and her labour under capitalism', *New Left Review*, vol. 83, pp. 3-24.

Secombe, W. (1975), 'Domestic labour—reply to critics', *New Left Review*, vol. 94, pp. 85-96.

Shils, E. (1966), 'Privacy: its constitution and vicissitudes', *Law and Contemporary Problems*, vol. 31, pp. 281-306.

Sillitoe, K. K. (1969), *Planning for Leisure* (London: HMSO).

Skolnick, A. (1973), *The Intimate Environment: Exploring Marriage and the Family* (Boston, Mass.: Little, Brown).

Slack, C. M. F. and Page, G. L. (1969), 'A contented profession?', *British Dental Journal*, vol. 127, pp. 220-9.

Smelser, N. J. (1972), *Social Change and the Industrial Revolution* (London: Routledge & Kegan Paul).

Sofer, C. (1970), *Men in Mid-Career* (Cambridge: Cambridge University Press).

Szalai, A. (ed.) (1972) *The Use of Time* (The Hague: Mouton).

Thompson, E. P. (1968), *The Making of the English Working Class* (Harmondsworth: Penguin).

Timperley, S. R. and Gregory, A. M. (1971), 'Some factors affecting the career choice and career perceptions of sixth form school leavers', *Sociological Review*, vol. 19, pp. 95-114.

Toomey, D. M. (1971), 'Conjugal roles and social networks in an urban working class sample', *Human Relations*, vol. 24, pp. 417-31.

Tunstall, J. (1966), *Old and Alone, a Sociological Study of Old People* (London: Routledge & Kegan Paul).

Turner, C. (1967), 'Conjugal roles and social networks: a re-examination of an hypothesis', *Human Relations*, vol. 20, pp. 121-30.

Turner, R. H. (1970), *Family Interaction* (New York: Wiley).

Veblen, T. (1899), 'The barbarian status of women', *American Journal of Sociology*, vol. 4, pp. 503-14.

Veblen, T. (1970), *The Theory of the Leisure Class* (London: Unwin Books).

Vollmer, H. M. and Mills, D. L. (eds) (1966), *Professionalization* (Englewood Cliffs, NJ: Prentice-Hall).

Watson, W. (1964), 'Social mobility and social class in industrial communities', in *Closed Systems and Open Minds*, ed. M. Gluckmann and E. Devons (Edinburgh: Oliver & Boyd), pp. 129-57.

Wainwright, H. (1978), 'Women and the division of labour', in *Work, Urbanism and Inequality*, ed. P. Abrams (London: Weidenfeld & Nicolson), pp. 160-205.

Weber, M. (1961), *From Max Weber: Essays in Sociology*, ed. H. H. Gerth and C. W. Mills (London: Routledge & Kegan Paul).

Weber, M. (1964), *The Theory of Social and Economic Organisation* (London: Collier Macmillan).

Weber, M. (1976), *The Protestant Ethic and the Spirit of Capitalism* (London: Allen & Unwin).

White, C. (1970), *Women's Magazines 1963-1968: A Sociological Study* (London: Michael Joseph).

Whyte, W. H. (1961), *The Organization Man* (Harmondsworth: Penguin).

Willmott, P. (1969), 'Some social trends', *Urban Studies*, vol. 6, pp. 286-308.

Willmott, P. and Young, M. (1967), *Family and Class in a London Suburb* (London: New English Library).

Wimberley, H. (1973), 'Conjugal role organisation and social networks in Japan and England', *Journal of Marriage and the Family*, vol. 35, pp. 125-30.

Winch, R. F. (1971), *The Modern Family* (New York: Holt, Rinehart & Winston).

Young, M. (1952), 'Distribution of income within the family', *British Journal of Sociology*, vol. 3, pp. 305-21.

Young, M. and Willmott, P. (1962), *Family and Kinship in East London* (Harmondsworth: Penguin).

Young, M. and Willmott, P. (1973), *The Symmetrical Family* (London: Routledge & Kegan Paul).

Zaretsky, E. (1976), *Capitalism, the Family and Personal Life* (London: Pluto Press).

Index

After-hours conjugal pattern 14
America, marital equality in 9, 56, 57

Burgesses 2, 37
  defined 1

Career; decisions on 61
  disappointment 95-6
  effect on moving house 61, 62
  families and leisure activities 83
  mobility 38
Cars, decision-making for 58, 63
Child-care: activities in conjugal sharing 7, 10
  preferences 93
  couples with a joint pattern 46-9
  husband's behaviour 104; *see also* Husband
  tasks 35, 36, 39; jointness in 40
Child-oriented leisure time 80
Child-rearing, jointness in 7, 40
  sharing tasks of 7, 40
Children, care of, for affluent couples 23
  clothes for, decision-making 58
  education of, decision-making for 58
  as leisure interest 81
Conjugal: family sex-role differentiation 18
  power and authority 53-71
  role(s) 68; jointness/equality 11; patterning, 29; among professional workers 33
  relationship 1-16; after-hours 14; case studies 13-16; influences affecting 2; joint 5; jointness in 6, 7, 9, 11; and marital equality 7; methods of calculation 11, 12; patterning of 5, 26; of salaried professional workers 1; segregation factors 6, 7, 9, 24, 104; and household division of labour 35-52; in domestic and child-care tasks 36, 41; and leisure interests 41; occupational career influences 38; three degrees of 35, 36
  spiralists 2, 37
  See also Marital
Contraception enabling wives to go out to work 9
Couples with a joint pattern of child-care

Couples, *cont.*
  behaviour 46
  with a segregate household division of labour 42-5
Critical anchorage 90, 91

Decision-making 104
  cars 58, 63
  children's education 58, 62
  conjugal sharing 7, 8, 9, 10
  family 53
  husband and 57, 61, 63, 67-8; work-career and 61, 62
  importance, frequency and pattern in family life 58ff
  veto in 68
  wives and 60-3
Demarcation disputes in the home 64, 65
Dentists and aspects of work 94-5
  effect of work on family life 31
  and leisure 78
  in sexual division of labour 27
Dependence on conjugal roles 29
Domestic: labour, value of 102
  tasks, behaviour 35; in conjugal sharing 7, 10; husband participation 36; oppression of 8
  work experiences 90-103; participation 74, 84
Dual-career couples, division of labour and responsibilities 25
  family problems 101-2

Earnings gap between men and women 25
Economic: life, domination of family life 31
  and social dependence, effect on women 98
Employee identification with work organisations 27
Employment of wives, difficulty of choices 99-101
  permission of husband for 29, 99, 101, 105
Equality: of marital power and authority 53, 54, 56, 57
  with marriage 7
  of opportunity, limitations of 19